Move Your... "But"

A JOURNEY INTO GOD'S HEART

Rose Hunter

TRILOGY CHRISTIAN PUBLISHERS
TUSTIN, CA

Trilogy Christian Publishers
A Wholly Owned Subsidary of Trinity Broadcasting Network
2442 Michelle Drive
Tustin, CA 92780

Manufactured in the United States of America

10 9 8 7 6 5 4 3 2 1

Library of Congress Cataloging-in-Publication Data is available.

ISBN: 978-1-64773-271-4

E-ISBN: 978-1-64773-272-1

Contents

Introduction

Love can't be fully understood analytically or rationally, and I suspect what trips us up in finding and living out true love is our human "default" setting to love each other conditionally: I love you if you..., I love you when you..., I love you because you..., and I love you until you...Flying in the face of conditional love is God's emphatic "I love you regardless!"

Human relationships seem to operate in three directions: outward toward others, upward toward God, and inward in relationship with our true, and sometimes unexplored, self. All three combine in a fully lived life, but it's difficult to navigate life with all three in mind, much less in balance. This prayer journal moves through those three directions: exploring who I truly am to God, exploring who God is as both Lord and Father, and exploring how I relate to others.

You will quickly notice this prayer journal is not of the "God is in the flowers, bunnies, and rainbows" flavor. In fact, although my friends and family know me for my sense of humor and the antic lengths I'll go just to drive home a point about the God who loves us through Jesus, and although I was known in my job at the Phoenix Zoo for the silly songs I wrote for children's programs, this book was born out of a long season of deep trials and tragedy I faced that challenged everything I believe about God's goodness, and from staring myself squarely in the face with truth in the middle of the storm.

Frankly, I find little comfort in stress-busting books that advise me to take a bubble bath, think positive thoughts, take a walk, or have my nails done to banish all my cares. God is in the flowers and rabbits and rainbows, maybe in the pedicure I had with my buddy Patty (but only because of Patty, not the polish), and probably in bubbles, too, but I need a God I can find within pain, loss, anxiety, disappointments, grief, and frustrations—God beside me. If God isn't great enough to be encountered and experienced there, in the darkness and tears, then what hope do any of us have for navigating real life?

Out of my analytical side, after I take the bubble bath and have my nails done, what has changed? Have those fun exercises changed my circumstances? Have they changed me? I love bubble baths, but I need something more substantial in my life; particularly, I need to see God's hand moving in me, beside me, to transform me in the middle of the messes I inadvertently step into like gum in a parking lot.

Out of my emotional side, I long to dance in the rain, not because I'm a pessimist, but because I know: rain will come. I need a God who isn't afraid to get wet beside me, who can transcend, transfigure, translate, and transform, as the lyrics in John Mark McMillan's moving, anointed song "How He Loves" powerfully declare: "When all of a sudden, I am unaware of these afflictions eclipsed by glory, and I realize just how beautiful You are and how great Your affections are for me." I need a God of grit and guts and glory. That's whom I'm encountering in this deepest trial of my life—a God of incredibly deep compassion and love—and that's whom I pray you will find within these thoughts and discoveries of mine.

If your life is sunshine, bunnies, and rainbows, then I hope you can find more joy as you travel through these pages in what God's spirit speaks to you each day. If your life is buffeted by trials, losses, grief, questions, and other hard realities that come with living in a world of broken people, then I hope you can find comfort, courage, love, and hope in these pages and, most importantly, in what God's spirit speaks to you personally each day as you listen.

The blank lines in each day's reading are for your own thoughts, cries, and situations and to create a place in your day where God can speak to your heart. Yes, God has a heart, and God wants to speak to you!

You matter. God cares. He is powerful, miracle-working, but most of all, tirelessly pursuing and relentlessly loving you regardless. Come take your own journey and explore an amazing relationship with God upwardly, outwardly, and inwardly.

Your fellow traveler, Rose

Move Your... "But"

"Yes, Mom, but..."

"I will, Dad, but..."

Every parent knows these phrases are actually kid-speak for "No." "Yes, but..." is camouflage meant to disguise, "I don't want to, and this is why..." or "I won't, and this is why..." with a pretended agreement. The little word "but" is both a simple conjunction and a powerful word we use to negate and contrast. Significantly and subliminally, it shapes our thoughts and attitudes, raises our emotional fists for a fight, and rationalizes our bad behavior. More dangerously, "but" can place a gate in the way of God's blessings and our intimacy with Him. "But" dismisses whatever comes before it and zeroes in our emphasis and focus on what comes after it. Our "buts" become our priority and overshadow everything else. Our "buts" get in the way of our peace and contentment and even living faith-full lives.

Though I knew this intuitively as a parent, I never recognized the power of this little word in my own life until one day when I was complain—I mean, explaining to the Lord why I was feeling so unhappy with my circumstances: "Yes, we have friends here, but all the other people I care about are all the way across the country." No thunderous voice rang out from the heavens, but I heard distinctly in my mind a soft "Ahem," followed by a firm, "you need to move your 'but.'" Startled, I instinctively cried out loud, "What? What did You say? Was... was that you, God?"

A settled spot in my spirit told me it was God's spirit speaking to me. Once I recovered from my initial shock and confusion, I slowly realized that both halves of my complaint were true, but I was focusing on the second phrase and disregarding the first. Where I put my "but" profoundly influenced my attitude. It determined whether I would be grateful or miserable, agitated or at peace, doubting or believing. I understood that I had a choice to make. I had the liberty to choose where I would put my "but," my focus, my attitude, and, as a result, my faith.

All that truth bundled itself up in one simple shift: "You need to move your 'but'!"

Examine my complaint again and see the difference one small shift makes: "All the other people I care about are across the country, but we have good friends here."

In any circumstance, usually, more than one thing is true. Even in the worst of circumstances, one of those truths is always God's positive truth. Changing what comes after my "but" to God's truth, to what is in my situation working for good, puts my focus on what I have rather than on what I lack. It shows me God's faithfulness when things aren't going the way I expect or want. It makes my priority what is eternally true rather than what's of fleeting value. Maybe you can identify with one of my examples:

From: I know you're doing good things in my friend's life to show her you love her, but she doesn't recognize them.

To: I know my friend doesn't recognize them, but I know you're doing good things in her life to show her you love her.

From: I know I should and can respond with respect and love, but he always talks to me so sarcastically.

To: He talks to me so sarcastically, but I should and can respond with respect and love.

From: We do have a roof over our heads, but it's one repair after another lately.

To: It's one repair after another lately, but we do have a roof over our heads.

From: I know You have a plan for good, God, but I certainly don't understand how this fits in that plan.

To: I don't understand how this fits in Your plan, God, but I know You have a plan for good.

Do you see the difference? If I move my "but" in front of what's both true and positive, my focus will follow. You think that semantic shift doesn't really change anything? Oh, yes, it powerfully does! That move redirects my thoughts and attitudes, and my thoughts and attitudes influence how I live out my day.

"Okay," you say, "that's great, but [there's a "but"] you don't understand how bad my situation is. What if the only truth I have is negative? What if I don't have anything positive to move my but in front of?" Hey, I have some pretty stinky things going on in my life, so I understand where you're coming from. The truth is, life is sometimes downright awful, but the truth is also that we always have a true and positive "but" to make our priority and focus. I just learned I have no cartilage and such bad arthritis and bone spurs in my right wrist that I need hand surgery, and my left wrist will soon follow suit. Genetics strikes again! But my doctor and physical therapist are amazed that I have such mobility and strength in my right hand. Do you think it matters to my attitude and in my daily walk where I put that "but"?

If you think there can't possibly be a positive "but" in what you're facing, just look at these buts in the Bible:

"...but you, Lord, are a shield around me, my glory, the One who lifts my head" (Psalm 3:3).

"...but the needy will not always be forgotten, nor the hope of the afflicted ever perish" (Psalm 9:8).

"...but those who hope in the LORD will renew their strength" (Isaiah 40: 31).

"...but I [Jesus] will see you again and you will rejoice, and no one will take away your joy" (John 16:22).

"...but take heart! I [Jesus] have overcome the world" (John 16:33).

What I hear Jesus saying when He contrasts and asserts, "You have heard it said..., but I tell you..." is that life may seem like this, but with Jesus in the picture, it's actually like this: Jesus, all He means and does and is, is the positive truth always in every circumstance and relationship in my life.

Feel free to claim any of these buts for your own life today! Try a little experiment. First, think about something that's bugging you or putting a negative focus on your life. Look for a positive truth there, too, and flip those two truths in that circumstance in your life. Next, dare to claim one of Jesus's "buts" for what seems impossible or undoable.

A "but" to pray: Oh, Father God, how many times have I told You yes when in my heart, I meant, "no, please no"? How many times have You called me to some service or blessing when I've responded, "yes, but..."? Oh, I've missed more blessings and opportunities than I want to know about, but You don't count my sins against me now because Jesus is my righteousness and His blood cleanses me from all sins, even my "buts."

So today, despite my disobedience, Lord Jesus, You tell me, *"But I will* _____
_____ in your life."* Thank You that every day, every morning, Your mercies are new, and Your faithfulness remains, as You promise in Lamentations 3:22-23.

Okay, for practice, here are some "buts" I'm asking you to help me move:

_____ but _____
_____ but _____
_____ but _____

In Jesus's name, amen! Holy Spirit, I'm listening.

_____

Breathless from Relentless Love

How intimately our Father knows us! And oh, how He surprises me on a regular basis. Just when you think you have God's intentions tracked and figured out...

On New Year's Day, 2010, I thought I had been waiting in the dark and cold on "A" Mountain, the butte north of Arizona State University that overlooks the campus, for a prayer group to arrive so I could join them in prayer for the city, school, and state. I knew none of them. Pastor Yoo began the meeting with songs and Scripture and then asked us to pair off to pray. A woman nearer my age than the students in the group sat directly in front of the rock I perched on, so we made eye contact and held hands in prayer. As we chatted afterward, she told me she lived across town but wanted to get involved in a church she'd heard of on the east side of the valley. "Coincidentally," it was my church, and I knew immediately that this was a divine appointment. God directed me to "A" Mountain rather than the place I'd intended to go that morning, and now I knew it was to bless Jessica and connect her with our prayer team. We laughed and exchanged phone numbers so we could meet the next Sunday at church.

Four months later, I felt a prompting to call Jessica. I hadn't seen her at church for a long time, wondered how she was doing, and really wanted her prayers for my ongoing and seemingly headed for defeat battle for my husband's faith and our marriage. Honestly, I'd plunged into bouts of pain and despair deeper than I ever imagined I could endure. So much for trusting God ruthlessly, as Brennan Manning writes in his book *Ruthless Trust*. Had I only known then how I would need the ruthless love of Jesus one year later!

God's ruthless, relentless love is exactly what met and covered me on "A" Mountain, though I didn't know it at the time. I didn't know it till April 13, a day I was flat on the floor feeling totally abandoned and devastated by yet another sign that this war in and for my husband and our marriage was advancing ruthlessly toward defeat. I cried out, "Prayer, prayer, and guidance. Oh, God, let's be honest," I screamed, "Show me Your will! I need to hear You!" I reeled to the phone and dialed, forcing my voice to be calm.

"Hi, Jessica, it's Rose. How are you?"

"Rose, I've been thinking about you for weeks, but I thought you were probably too busy..." (Note to me: never assume anyone is too busy for me to call if God's spirit puts her/him on my mind!)

Thus began the conversation and prayer that totally changed my understanding of that New Year's Day encounter. In our initial catching up, Jessica related that she'd moved back across the valley and was at her former church. Hmmm...my brain started churning, *Then what was January 1 about?*

Jessica began praying for me, and out poured dark visions of my husband, visions of our younger son, and visions for me, including "I see you in God's arms. He cherishes you!"

I wish I'd had a pencil and paper with me that afternoon to record her words accurately! To say I was blown away is to understate the lifting in my heart. I do remember precisely her momentary pause, then this instruction: "God wants to give you a new outfit...He wants you to go buy a new outfit."

How funny, how unexpected that was, and how suddenly I recognized that back on January 1, 2011, Jesus knew I would need Jessica's insight and prayers on April 13! I thought I was there for her, but Jesus placed her there on that cold rock for me! I know God has maneuvered and moved me literally across the world to meet other people's very pointed and specific needs at pointed, specific times. Now He brought His love wrapped in another person to meet my heart's need.

He positions us to carry His word and love for someone else and puts us in the right places at the right times to be part of what God Almighty is doing! But to experience Him doing that for me—how humbling, how powerful, what a profound sense of His loving and knowing and being more than able!

"Now this is what the LORD says—he who created you, O Jacob, he who formed you, O Israel: 'Fear not, for I have redeemed you; I have summoned you by name; you are mine'" (Isaiah 43:1).

"I am the good shepherd; I know my sheep and my sheep know me" (John 10:14).

Oh, to be known by the Creator of the universe, to be called *His*! Treasured, cherished, known!

So what did I do? Given the financial vise our joint checking account was in, I couldn't afford to splurge on a new dress, but the next day, after a doctor appointment, I went to a local thrift store and found a spectacular crimson, gauzy, ankle-length dress embroidered with gold thread and gold sequins for—drum roll please—$6.99. I wore it the next weekend while I presented the Sunday morning devotional message at a women's retreat, testifying to the truth that our Father knows us uniquely as individuals and *cares passionately* about us, uniquely as individuals, each as His one-in-a-billion beloved child. That dress restored broken hearts in the message I gave, too! Thank You, thank You again, Father!

He showed up for me the next week at a fountain on my job as an educator at the zoo as I waited for a very late high school group to show up for their rainforest tour. Many people passed me heading up the trail, but one woman with her husband stopped and turned to me, "Rose...Mary...Rose?" Fourteen years since I'd seen her, but I recognized Jan immediately! She'd moved out of the valley and lived about a hundred miles north. Amazed, we hugged in a joyful reunion. We had a wonderful time reconnecting and praying right there in the middle of traffic, and, to top it off, she and her husband were great friends of the brother of the pastor who was counseling my husband and me.

How intricately God weaves His will into our lives! What are the odds? Spot on when Jesus is at work loving and knowing me. What does this mean for you? He knows you, truly knows you, and is already at work to meet your deepest heart needs with His ruthless, relentless, mighty, able, and more-than-willing love.

Yes, I believe in miracles...even when the answer is different from the hope I held, God holds me in His love.

A "but" to pray: Oh, Father, how many times have You moved me into place or sent someone into my life, connected me with another out of Your great love? I'll bet I've missed seeing Your hand and love at work so many times. It's so easy for me to doubt Your love when difficult circumstances surround me, and sometimes during the nights I "sit in darkness on the mountain" waiting for help to come, I wonder if You've forgotten me. But help me remember Your promise that You could no more forget me than a mother could forget the baby at her breast. Show me where I should go today if I'm to be Your hand of love to someone or if You're sending someone to meet the need of my heart. Today my heart needs _____

_____from

you. Today I know You want me to be "Jesus with skin on" and give _____

encouragement by _____

_____. Don't let me fall or crawl out of Your arms! In Jesus's name, amen!

TransFiction or Transformation

I always get picked. Whenever we go to the Arizona Renaissance Festival or any stage show that involves audience participation, there must be a sign over my head that says, "Pick This One." With horror, I watch the performer's smile grow as his/her finger points my way, and I try to duck, but it never works. The next thing I know, I'm up on stage as "Sister Helena Handbasket" or, worse yet, "The Church Lady."

I cringe most recalling Old Tucson, the gray medicine wagon, and "Professor Magillicutty's Astounding TransFiction Show." That's where I became and confronted "The Church Lady." I still cringe because I felt so incredibly uncomfortable, far beyond the normal and expected embarrassment at being the object of poked fun. Embarrassment I could have handled. Conviction was another story. Why was I squirming inside? It was that word, "TransFiction."

There I was, chosen and branded probably because I looked inoffensive, good-natured, a bit gullible, and easily embarrassable, the Church Lady. I looked sweet on the outside, but that was fiction. My watching family knew all too well who I was inside, and the truth was that the inside didn't always match the appearance, tambourine or not. I don't remember specifically, but I'd probably just let a loved one have it with both barrels of my quick wit and my righteous indignation, or just agreed with someone I love out of a less than agreeable attitude, before the professor's assistant singled me out of the crowd. Tambourine rattling in my hand, in my head, I heard clearly, "If I speak with the tongues of men and of angels, but do not have love, I have become a noisy gong or a clanging cymbal" (1 Corinthians 13:1).

For me to stop sweating when I'm the local comedic color, for my inside to match my outside and TransFiction to become true transformation, I know I need more than a miracle elixir like Professor Magillicutty's snake oil (advertised in the sign on his wagon in the photo above to "Restore Your Love, Generate Good Health, and Improve Your Mental Processes). I need something truly effective. I need the mind of Christ. And I realize to have the mind of Christ, I need to have the heart of Jesus. What I'm thinking often determines how I'm feeling and vice versa. Stew on a perceived insult, and I cook up anger. Think about the feeling of joy I feel in holding my new granddaughter, and my thoughts turn to blessing and peace, transforming my words into words of blessing and validation toward my son and daughter-in-law. Thoughts, emotions, attitudes, and words powerfully interact. Change my thoughts, and I can change my feelings and words.

May I create a new corollary on Jesus's words from Matthew 6:21 (KJV), "Where your treasure is, there will your heart be also"? Where your thoughts go, there will your emotions and words and actions go also.

In her book *Battlefield of the Mind,* Joyce Meyer says, "We would make tremendous progress simply by learning how to discern life and death."[1] Oh, *that's* easy! Sometimes the attitude poison flies out of my mouth disguised as correction or wise advice before I realize I'm spitting destruction. Sometimes, sadly, I've thought about it. Oh, that I *could* discern life and death before I let fly!

Astoundingly, though, you and I have hope and assurance that we can and that we can be transformed from "church ladies" (or men) to disciples. God promises: "I will give you a new heart and put a new spirit in you; I will remove from you your heart of stone and give you a heart of flesh. And I will put my Spirit in you" (Ezekiel 36:26-27).

> But Christ has blessed you with the Holy Spirit. Now the Spirit stays in you [...] The Spirit is truthful and teaches you everything. So stay one in your heart with Christ, just as the Spirit has taught you to do.
>
> 1 John 2:27 (CEV)

"The mind of sinful man is death, but the mind controlled by the Spirit is life and peace" (Romans 8:6).

God's spirit in us is the difference between death and life, church lady and disciple; I want to be a disciple.

> A disciple, or apprentice, is simply someone who has decided to be with another person, under appropriate conditions, in order to become capable of doing what that person does or to become what that person is [...] I am not necessarily learning to do everything he [Jesus] did, but I am learning how to do everything I do in the manner that he did all that he did.[2]

Apprentices learn techniques, but being Jesus's apprentice/disciple isn't about learning a technique or about swallowing a magic elixir, it's about having His heart and learning to love with His love. In my prayer time over the past year as I've asked Jesus to show me what's on His heart for people in my life, and as I focused on personal repentance to get ready for Reign-Down USA's national day of repentance on April 8, 2008, Jesus has done and is doing a work of real transformation in me. Love is coming to life in my heart in places I feared were beyond love's resurrection. I'm even catching hurtful words in the thought stage and taking those thoughts captive to make them obedient to Christ (2 Corinthians 10:5).

The wonderful thing about the relationship with Jesus, God with us in humanity, Emmanuel, is that Jesus called His disciples exactly where they were, in their human limitations and weaknesses, but He didn't leave them in that state. Walking beside them, mere men, He poured Himself into them to lead them to a higher life and calling. On the day of Pentecost, God poured His Holy Spirit into Jesus' followers in the Upper Room to lift their love, vision, compassion, and calling even higher. He truly turned fishermen, tax collectors, and everyday people into fishers of men, empowered with God's spirit to do much more than they ever dared dream they could do: heal the sick, drive out evil spirits, preach, pray, and exhort with compelling, passionate power, lead men and women to Jesus, and raise the dead.

Even more than controlling our tongues, although that is a huge miracle in itself, Jesus gave His command to His disciples to go and be His hands, feet, voice, heart, mind, and authority here on the earth.

> The seventy-two returned with joy and said, "Lord, even the demons submit to us in your name." He replied, "I saw Satan fall like lightning from heaven. I have given you authority to trample on snakes and scorpions and to overcome all the power of the enemy; nothing will harm you. However, do not rejoice that the spirits submit to you, but rejoice that your names are written in heaven."
>
> Luke 10:17-20

> As Jesus was walking beside the Sea of Galilee, he saw two brothers, Simon called Peter and his brother Andrew. They were casting a net into the lake, for they were fishermen. "Come, follow me," Jesus said, "and I will send you out to fish for people." At once they left their nets and followed him.
>
> Matthew 4:18-20

> Most assuredly, I say to you, he who believes in me, the works that I do he will do also; and greater works than these he will do, because I go to My Father. And whatever you ask in my

name, that I will do, that the Father may be glorified in the Son. If you ask anything in my name, I will do it.

John 14:12-14 (NKJV)

As you go, proclaim this message: "The kingdom of heaven has come near." Heal the sick, raise the dead, cleanse those who have leprosy, drive out demons. Freely you have received; freely give.

Matthew 10:7-8

"And these signs will follow those who believe: In My name they will cast out demons; they will speak with new tongues; they will take up serpents; and if they drink anything deadly, it will by no means hurt them; they will lay hands on the sick, and they will recover." So then, after the Lord had spoken to them, He was received up into heaven, and sat down at the right hand of God.

Mark 16:17-19 (NKJV)

Gosh, what a relief—no, what a victory—to know that what I think doesn't *have* to come out of my mouth and wound spirits of others! No more "Church Lady"! And amazingly, I've seen Jesus's words prove true when

I've prayed with neighbors, friends, and even complete strangers and seen a transformation in their lives. I will never forget the afternoon my neighbor Lisa came to my front door, crying about her rebellious teenage son Hector, who was in trouble with the law again. I prayed, simply prayed, for Hector, for Lisa, and the family. Honestly, I didn't feel a thing except compassion, but Lisa's eyes widened in joy, and she said, "I just felt something leave me, something heavy just left my brain!" It took another year, but Hector turned his life around. I'm no one special or extraordinary; I'm just an ordinary woman who loves Jesus and others, believes God wants me to be His hands, feet, and heart here on the earth, and I accept the opportunities God places in my daily life to bring His Spirit into the lives of others.

The sign on Professor Magillicutty's medicine wagon can become truth, not fiction, for all of us. With His own Spirit and His "heart of flesh," Jesus will restore our love, generate good health, improve our mental processes, and as a special bonus, even equip us to do the works He did! We have authority, power, presence, and love beyond any magic elixir when Christ dwells richly in our hearts through faith.

A "but" for you to move/pray today, and room for you to ask Jesus to reveal another "but" to you: God, I know sometimes and in some places and relationships my "Christlikeness" has been fiction, not truth. I remem-

ber the time I _____,
but I know and believe You can and will transform me
because Your Word promises that You will take away
my heart of stone and give me a heart of flesh, Jesus's
very own heart, and put Your Spirit in me. I give You
the freedom to show me where I need to repent in my
attitudes and whom I need to love with Your love. "__
_____." Thank
You that from today forward, I don't have to live a life
of "Astounding TransFiction," but a real transformation in my life and even, when I'm just obedient to the
need of the moment, transformation in the lives of
other people! In Jesus's name, amen! Holy Spirit, I'm
listening.

_____

Keep Off the Grass?

One of our funniest family moments at Disneyland was during the "Year of a Million Dreams." I hoped to get a special treat for my younger son, Ethan's twenty-first birthday, something like a free pass or free Fast-Passes or a dinner somewhere. He was aiming for a job with Disney (which now, praise God, he has), so the best birthday present I could think of for him was a behind-the-scenes "Walk in Walt's Footsteps" guided tour.

Our tour guide Lani was so much animated fun (yes, that's an intentional Disney pun), and she practically adopted Ethan as her own with all the jolly bantering they did back and forth. We stopped and stood inside a fenced-off grassy area to view Sleeping Beauty Castle while Lani told us about its history. Suddenly, the thought struck Ethan and me about how funny it would be if he could lie down in the grass because attached to the fence around the small plot was a "Keep Off the Grass" sign. Lani leaped into the fun, offering him the privilege as his "dream" for the day, and we snapped a hilarious photo of her shaking her riding crop at Ethan as he lounged in the lawn with the sign clearly visible behind him.

What fun! It broke the whole tour group into hilarity, and I can imagine Walt Disney himself would have smiled at the polite irreverence. So I wonder: does God have "Keep Off the Grass" signs in heaven? I doubt it! And one reason I'm sure the King of Kings and Lord of Lords isn't that stuffy is an encounter I had one morning in my quiet time. Curled up crosswise in my blue wing chair as though sitting in my father's lap, I envisioned climbing in the boughs of a large, leafy tree. I loved to climb trees as a child and still do if the branches are accommodating. As I "saw" myself sitting on a limb, I sensed I "saw" someone else sitting on a branch not far from me. To my startled delight, I realized it was Jesus, up in a tree, smiling and laughing!

"Well, of course," I said in my thoughts, "you were a fully human boy down here. You drew pictures in the dirt, maybe made mud pies, played games with your brothers and sisters (Matthew 13:55-56 names James, Joseph [Joses], Judas [Jude], and Simon Jesus's brothers and mentions unnamed sisters.), tried to catch butterflies, skipped stones on the Sea of Galilee. Of course, you liked to climb trees!"

Then a wondrous realization began to dawn in me. I wasn't sitting in just any tree; I was perched in the branches of the tree of life John wrote about in the book of Revelation:

> Then he showed me a river of the water of life, clear as crystal, coming from the throne of God and of the Lamb, in the middle of its street. On either side of the river was the tree of life, bearing twelve kinds of fruit, yielding its fruit every month; and the leaves of the tree were for the healing of the nations.
>
> Revelation 22:1-2 (NASB)

"Wow!" was all I could breathe, awash in amazement at the intimacy, the warm, understanding, identifying love in my Savior.

"For we do not have a high priest who is unable to sympathize with our weaknesses, but one who in every respect has been tempted as we are, yet without sin" (Hebrews 4:15, ESV).

And I knew the river blowing below me at the base of the tree. A year earlier, I woke up on my birthday in a lovely resort in Thailand to help there in the vacation Bible school program a church in Texas had brought for over a hundred children of the missionaries meeting at the conference center. I awoke in the middle of dreaming Jesus was offering me a cup of water he'd just dipped from a river. I knew it was His life in the cup and in the river. Completely unashamed, I asked Jesus if I could dip my hand, then my head in a barrel of that water, and then instantly, scandalously unashamed, I cried out, "No, I want to jump in the river! I want to dive in it, swim in it, splash in it!"

Can the almighty God who spoke the universe into existence, "He who is the blessed and only Sovereign, the King of kings and Lord of lords, who alone has immortality, who dwells in unapproachable light, whom no one has ever seen or can see" (1 Timothy 6:15-16, ESV), possibly tolerate such childlike joy and trust from His child? More than tolerate our childlike love, I suspect God exults in it and in the requests we make out of abandoned trust in His love!

"Father of Lights," the Vineyard song by John Barnett says, "You delight in Your children. Every good and perfect gift comes from you."[3]

> Don't be deceived, my dear brothers and sisters. Every good and perfect gift is from above, coming down from the Father of the heavenly lights, who does not change like shifting shadows. He chose to give us birth through the word of truth that we might be a kind of firstfruits of all he created.
>
> James 1:16-18

"The LORD takes pleasure in those who fear him, in those who hope in his steadfast love" (Psalm 147:11, ESV).

"For the LORD takes pleasure in His people; He will beautify the afflicted ones with salvation" (Psalm 148:4, NASB).

> "but let him who boasts boast of this, that he understands and knows Me, that I am the LORD who exercises lovingkindness, justice and righteousness on earth; for I delight in these things," declares the LORD.
>
> Jeremiah 8:24 (NASB)

God knows what delights each one of us. Climbing trees and splashing in a river delight me; why wouldn't God, who delights in my love for His love for me, indulge me in something that gives glory to His faithful, intimately knowing love?

- Psalm 37:4 (ESV), *"Delight yourself in the LORD,* and he will give you the desires of your heart."
- Philippians 4:4 (ESV), *"Rejoice in the Lord always;* again I will say, rejoice."
- Romans 5:2 (ESV), "Through him we have also obtained access by faith into this grace in which we stand, and *we rejoice in hope of the glory of God."*
- Psalm 43:4 (ESV), "Then I will go to the altar of God, to God *my exceeding joy."*
- Psalm 70:4 (ESV), "May all who seek you rejoice and be glad in you! May those who love your salvation say evermore, 'God is great!'"
- Psalm 63:3 (ESV), "Because your steadfast love is better than life, my lips will praise you."

Why do we think our quiet times with the Lord have to be sober, somber, deeply "religious" moments? Can't we enjoy God? Can't we take the Holy Spirit's hand and run through a field of flowers? Can't I join in the circle dancing a grapevine step with Jesus to הליגנ הבה, *Havah Nagilah,* "Let us rejoice"? Can't I marvel at the iridescence and improbability of a hummingbird hovering outside my window and wonder how those tiny wings beat so fast, and marvel and laugh with the Creator who designed them? Can't I lay on the expanse of grass in New Jerusalem and laugh that the sign says, "Please, wiggle your toes in the grass to your hearts' delight"?

In these verses, I rest my case on the luxuriant lawn of God's lavish love. Our Father delights in His children delighting in Him!

> Oh, magnify the LORD with me, and let us exalt his name together! I sought the LORD, and he answered me and delivered me from all my fears. Those who look to him are radiant, and their faces shall never be ashamed. This poor man cried, and the LORD heard him and saved him out of all his troubles. The angel of the LORD encamps around those who fear him, and delivers them. Oh, taste and see that the LORD is good! Blessed is the man who takes refuge in him! Oh, fear the LORD, you his saints, for those who fear him have no lack! The young lions suffer want and hunger; but those who seek the LORD lack no good thing.
>
> Psalm 34:3-10 (ESV)

Delight yourself in the LORD, and he will give you the desires of your heart. Commit your way to the LORD; trust in him, and he will act. He will bring forth your righteousness as the light, and your justice as the noonday.

Psalm 37:4-7 (ESV)

A "but" to pray: Father God, You truly have a father's heart! I'm human, limited, and it's impossible for me to keep Your awesome holiness in mind; at the same time, I press into Your arms in intimate confident love, *but* I know You understand, so here it goes: if I could reach back into the things I loved as a child and do anything I wanted to do, virtually, in heaven today, I'd love to ____

_____

_____

_____. I'd love to see You there, enjoying the fun with me. How would You like to have fun in my life today? Together let's break the "act like an adult" rules and _____

_____! I love You, Father, and I love Your love for me, all of me, even the child still inside me. In Jesus's name, amen. Holy Spirit, I'm listening on my string and paper cup telephone.

_____

Two Brown Shoes Don't Make a Pair

One typical hectic December Saturday conspired against my getting ready for a formal dinner on time, but I learned something valuable about Jesus in the discount store mêlée. After a chiropractor appointment all the way across town, we stopped into two stores, then the markdown outlet of a famous retailer to look for a demure jacket I could wear with the long strapless dress I planned to wear for that night's workplace Christmas dinner. I would have compromised my Christian witness wearing that dress sans jacket!

Walking through the shoe section with me in my aerobic shopping mode, my husband spied a cute pair of short brown boots. No, they weren't what I was looking for, but I had said I wanted a pair. As I picked them up to find the price tag, I saw a deal simply too good to pass up. Untie tennis shoes, whip them off, put on boots, lace halfway to be sure they fit, bingo, put tennis shoes back on, boots in hand, dash through dress section, no luck, pay for shoes, enter store #4, find the jacket, dash home, fix dinner for kids, shower, dress, and leave for our dinner across town. Have a fun time.

One month later, after I'd worn the brown boots many times, I noticed the left one didn't feel as comfy. Something about the cuff on the shoe bothered my left ankle. I took off my shoes and really looked at them; I mean, I *really* looked at them and was dumbfounded. They weren't the same shoe! They were the same color, had the same toe, same laces, *but* there the resemblance ended. The right shoe was topstitched with a single row of stitching outside the eyelets, but the left one was topstitched with a double row of stitching *inside* the eyelets. The right shoe had a cuff; the left had a padded top like a hiking boot. I'd been wearing two different shoes for a month and never knew it!

I was totally embarrassed. Now, what should I do? I couldn't take them back because the markdown outlet was named Last Chance for a reason: you bought it, it's yours forever, no returns or exchanges.

The lesson to me? Close isn't close enough. Besides taking time to be sure the shoes I buy are truly a matched pair, I recognized that sometimes what people believe or say about Jesus is inconsistent, doesn't match up with the truth of who He is. Sometimes my thoughts about God don't match up with His true character revealed in the Bible. And sometimes, my words and actions aren't consistent with the Christian life I say I live.

When I live inconsistently with my faith, I feel as uncomfortable as I did wearing two different shoes!

Regarding Jesus, some of my acquaintances assure me they believe Jesus was a good man, maybe the best man to ever walk the earth. But they quickly point out that everyone has his or her own path to God, that there must be more than one way because so many people think there is, and who could possibly believe all those educated people are in error, especially when some of them do go to church.

Match that "shoe" against what the Bible says about Jesus, and what Jesus said about Himself:

> Thomas said to Him, "Lord, we do not know where you are going, how do we know the way?" Jesus said to him, "I am the way, and the truth, and the life; no one comes to the Father but through me."
> "If you had known me, you would have known My Father also; from now on you know Him, and have seen Him."
> Philip said to Him, "Lord, show us the Father, and it is enough for us." Jesus said to him, "Have I been so long with you, and yet you have not come to know Me, Philip? He who

has seen me has seen the Father; how can you say, 'Show us the Father'? Do you not believe that I am in the Father, and the Father is in me? The words that I say to you I do not speak on my own initiative, but the Father abiding in me does His works. Believe Me that I am in the Father and the Father is in me; otherwise believe because of the works themselves."

John 14:5-11 (NASB)

"The Word became flesh and made his dwelling among us. We have seen his glory, the glory of the one and only Son, who came from the Father, full of grace and truth" (John 1:14).

"I am the gate; whoever enters through me will be saved. They will come in and go out, and find pasture" (John 10:9).

Jesus answered, "I did tell you, but you do not believe. The works I do in my Father's name testify about me, but you do not believe because you are not my sheep. My sheep listen to my voice; I know them, and they follow me. I give them eternal life, and they shall never perish; no one will snatch them out of my hand. My Father, who has given them to me, is greater than all; no one can snatch them out of my Father's hand. I and the Father are one."

John 10:25-30

So the Jews said to Him, "You are not yet fifty years old, and have you seen Abraham?" Jesus said to them, "Truly, truly, I say to you, before Abraham was born, I am." Therefore they picked up stones to throw at Him, but Jesus hid himself and went out of the temple.

John 8:57-59 (ESV)

"God said to Moses, 'I AM WHO I AM. This is what you are to say to the Israelites: 'I AM has sent me to you'" (Exodus 3:14).

"Jesus said to her, 'I am the resurrection and the life. The one who believes in me will live, even though they die; and whoever lives and believes in me will never die'" (John 11:25).

In the beginning was the Word, and the Word was with God, and the Word was God. He was in the beginning with God. All things came into being through Him, and apart from Him nothing came into being that has come into being. In Him was life, and the life was the Light of men. The Light shines in the darkness, and the darkness did not comprehend it. [...] There was the true Light which, coming into the world, enlightens every man. He was in the world, and the world was made through Him, and the world did not know Him. He came to His own, and those who were His own did not receive Him. But as many as received Him, to them He gave the right to become children of God, even to those who believe in His name, who were born, not of blood nor of the will of the flesh nor of the will of man, but of God. And the Word became flesh, and dwelt among us, and we saw His glory, glory as of the only begotten from the Father, full of grace and truth.

John 1:1-5, 9-14 (NASB)

But what does it say? "THE WORD IS NEAR YOU, IN YOUR MOUTH AND IN YOUR HEART"—that is, the word of faith which we are preaching, that if you confess with your mouth Jesus as Lord, and believe in your heart that God raised Him from the dead, you will be saved; with the heart a person believes, resulting in righteousness, and with the mouth he confesses, resulting in salvation.

Romans 10:8-10 (NASB)

"I write these things to you who believe in the name of the Son of God so that you may know that you have eternal life" (1 John 5:13).

Jesus was just a good teacher, an enlightened man, a prophet, one good idea? Yes, He was a teacher, a good man, proclaiming prophetic Word, *but* I don't think that matches with His Lordship, *the* way, *the* truth, *the* life. Two brown shoes don't make a pair.

Regarding God's character, my image of God in confusing times is strikingly in opposition to what I believe about God when my life is going smoothly. In prosperous, healthier, joyful times, I gladly agree with the biblical writers who rejoiced in God's character:

"But you, O Lord, are a compassionate and gracious God, slow to anger, abounding in love and faithfulness" (Psalm 86:15).

"He is the Rock, his works are perfect, and all his ways are just. A faithful God who does no wrong, upright and just is he" (Deuteronomy 32:4).

"For the LORD is good and his love endures forever; his faithfulness continues through all generations" (Psalm 100:5).

"Taste and see that the LORD is good" (Psalm 34:8).

Taste and see...I think of my neighbor Alaine's crawfish étouffée. Many years ago, after eating a disgusting, multi-legged slice of a marine invertebrate during a trip to Asia, I made a resolution never to eat anything with less than two or more than four legs, so when Alaine brought over a steaming bowl of her signature Louisiana chowder, I cringed. I knew it couldn't possibly taste good. Too many legs in that bowl!

Since Alaine had gone to so much trouble to make it, though, what could I do but set it on the table and partake of her hospitality? I carefully tipped all but two crawfish off the spoon and back into the dish before ladling a serving onto my plate. Tentatively I bit into one, and...it actually didn't taste bad. It didn't taste wonderful to me, either it's the crawfish's art-gum eraser texture that throws me, but the non-crawfish part of the chowder was quite tasty. My husband and our son enjoyed the crawfish, though, and happily ate the rest of my share, which proves two things: first, one man's gastronomic challenge is another man's gusto, and second, there is goodness in things outside of my definition of "good." To put it another way: God's goodness may not always taste the way I think it should, but it still is goodness, and He is always and forever good.

Looking back through my journals to so many of the troubling times when I couldn't see any sign of God's goodness, again and again, I find good. We wanted two children, and timing them four years apart so we wouldn't have two kids in college at the same time just made good economic sense to me. However, it took seven years for me to conceive our second child: seven years of prayers and hope repeatedly dashed, till I almost gave up hoping before Ethan came along. Our sons were born eleven years apart, and in the year our younger son graduated from high school, our older son received his PhD. God answered my prayer with a yes; I just hadn't realized that eleven years would fit the timetable of my request perfectly!

After Ethan's birth, I also realized that any other child we might have conceived would not have been Ethan: a creative, compassionate, intelligent, honest, giving, loving, loyal, hard-working young man of faith and vision. Go through the Boy Scout oath, and that's Ethan. God had a specific purpose for that specific combination of DNA that is Ethan. That is goodness; that is love; that is faithfulness. The seven-year heartache of suspected infertility became a spoonful of goodness in the empathy I now have for women struggling with infertility.

Again and again, I remember crises and wrenching situations that became avenues of blessing on down the road: a treasured necklace lost, a lost diamond found, and acknowledging that the God who was good when I found the diamond was the same good God when I didn't find the necklace. My husband was laid off and out of work for six months, and a loving God connected him with a job better than he applied for. A cross-country move I didn't want to make away from everyone and everything I cherished, and through that frustrating move when I thought He had abandoned me, God twice met desperate needs my kids and I would have years later. That's goodness. That's faithfulness. That's love. That's the true character of God the Father.

In difficult times, is it God who is inconstant, or my emotions and my thinking that don't line up with truth and can't be trusted? I open my Bible to psalm eighty-nine, to the words of another Ethan, "the Ezrahite," and I stand on this "but":

> I will sing of the LORD's great love forever; [...] I will declare that your love stands firm forever, that you established your faithfulness in heaven itself. [...] Blessed are those who have learned to acclaim you, who walk in the light of your presence, LORD. [...] For you are their glory and strength.
>
> Psalm 89:1-2, 15, 17

Today I make a choice to believe *Jesus is the Lord* and to believe God's character, not the economy, not my arthritis, not the circumstances around us, and I will walk in those matching shoes believing God's love, kindness, compassion, and power till I get to the place where I can turn and see we've been surrounded by His goodness all the while.

A "but" to pray: Loving Father, I look at all the problems, discouraging news, financial losses, and uncertainties around me, but I trust that You love us, You never forsake me, Your will is for our good, and You are faithfully working out blessing even when I can't see You. Today I see _____

_____, but/and I believe that you are truly _____

_____. Show me where what I believe is inconsistent with the truth of who You are, Jesus. _____

_____

_____

Thank you that I'll look back in a few days, weeks, or years and rejoice in what You are doing to work all of this "chowder" together for my good through Your steadfast, mighty wisdom, provision, and love. I *will* taste and see Your goodness! "I am confident of this: I will see the goodness of the LORD in the land of the living" (Psalm 27:13). I will wait for you, Lord; I will be strong and take heart and wait for You, Lord (see Psalm 27:14). In Jesus's name, amen. Holy Spirit, I'm listening.

_____

Whose Blood Bought Me?

How I treasure those brief flashes of deep, gut insight that hit me much less frequently than I long for. Do you know what I mean? Times when you feel for a nanosecond that you've touched a deep truth about God, and you wish with everything in you that it would engulf you so you could immerse yourself in its power? Frustratingly, those moments never linger long enough.

The latest one that grazed my consciousness on Palm Sunday, March 24, entered the orbit of my subconscious during the week before as I searched YouTube for some exciting video and information about relative sizes of objects in space for the third-grade class I assist in. Some facts about VY Canis Majoris absolutely astounded me: a red hypergiant, it's one of the largest stars we know of, with a diameter of 1,227,000,000 miles (that's a billion, if you don't want to count the place value yourself), or 1,975,000,000 kilometers. Its mass is thirty times that of our sun, and it is 4,892 light-years from Earth.

To give you a better sense of that immensity, if VY Canis Majoris was at the center of our solar system, its surface would extend at least beyond the orbit of Jupiter and perhaps as far as the orbit of Saturn. What grabbed my attention in the video was the comment that if you could fly in a jet at 900 miles per hour, it would take you over 1,000 years to fly around the star! It's so distant that the light of VY Canis Majoris takes 3,9000 years to reach us.

I sat in bed at 5 a.m. that Sunday and tried to cold-start praising the King of Kings as Holy Week began. A realization rose slightly above the horizon of my consciousness: *whose* blood bought me? *Whose* blood? Yes, Jesus's blood—that rolls of my tongue almost tritely sometimes—but *what* blood is His?

"And God said, 'Let there be lights in the expanse of the sky to separate the day from the night,' [...] And it was so. God made two great lights [...] He also made the stars" (Genesis 1:14-16).

"Where were you when I laid the earth's foundation? [...] On what were its footings set, or who laid its cornerstone—while the morning stars sang together and all the angels shouted for joy?" (Job 38:4, 6-7)

"He determines the number of the stars and calls them each by name" (Psalm 147:4).

"In the beginning was the Word, and the Word was with God and the Word was God [...] Through him all things were made; without him nothing was made that has been made" (John 1:1, 3).

"I, Jesus, [...] am the Root, and the Offspring of David, and the bright Morning Star" (Revelation 22:16).

The "gestalt" of the physics of VY Canis Majoris fused with these Bible verses and blazed into a whole much bigger than the sum of its parts. The blood that bled for every speck of sin in my life coursed through the veins of the One whose voice spoke the inferno of VY Canis Majoris into existence. That blood! The most precious fluid and outrageous gift in the universe because it was the blood of the One who imagined, then spoke blood into being, and who bound the vastness of Himself within the confines of a completely human body to spill His blood instead of requiring mine.

And He willingly gave it for me.

Oh, I wanted to grasp the enormity of that love in every cell of my body and neuron of my understanding! Like a meteorite, infinite love tore through the atmosphere of my finite comprehension. Why in the world do I think I'm not loved? Why do we think we have to, or ever could, earn that love? And engulfed by that love, why in the universe am I ever afraid?

His eyes are like blazing fire, and on his head are many crowns [...] and his name is the Word of God [...] On his robe and on his thigh he has this name written: KING OF KINGS AND LORD OF LORDS!

Revelation 19:12, 13, 16

Even now I feel like I'm writing a plasma breath of truth with hands and understanding of concrete, but, O God, let me burn with that reality one day! Brand my heart with it now: I am Yours!

A "but" to pray: Oh, Lord God, I am *Yours!* I, *I* am Yours. I *am* Yours! Some days I get so caught up in the details and urgencies of living that I live as though You aren't even "there," *but* who are You?

_____. I want to truly know You, to truly experience who You are. I want to

_____.

Holy Spirit, give me a true, deep revelation of how immense God is. Overcome my finiteness for even a few seconds as I think about the vastness of Your greatness

_____. And You thought, You think I'm worth reaching across time and space to reveal Your Son Jesus to me! Lord, I'm amazed! Show me more of who You are. In Jesus's name, amen. Holy Spirit, I'm listening.

DAY 7

Trophy Bride

I often prayed to really experience God's love for me, to move knowledge of God's love from my head to an experienced reality in my gut. So many of my friends seemed to slip so easily into God's heart, like stepping into a beautiful ball gown (the sanguine friends) or sliding into a soft, voluminous cashmere sweater (my fellow melancholics), but I never imagine what life would throw at me to send me into God's unquenchable love.

Maybe I'm so analytical that it took agony to override my analysis, or maybe, like with Job in the Bible, the enemy just asked to sift me, or maybe it's just that we live in a fallen world where people with free will do hurtful things to each other. Haven't I unintentionally done things that hurt others? I grew up in a pretty normal Christian home where my mother and father spoke kindly to each other, showed affection, and never shared a cross word in front of us kids. Even my older brother, younger sister, and I got along together with few conflicts and quarrels to ruffle our sense of belonging. Then I left home, got married, and walked straight into what I didn't know at the time was a duo of serious personality disorders in another human being wounded by his family.

Whatever the reason, we struggle with the concept of God's love. Unless you have found yourself a "castaway" adrift in a sea of the loss of what or who you once loved or of all you hoped for, you probably can't comprehend an utter emptiness that feels deeper than death, and the resulting desperate longing that compels you directly into the flame of the blazing, ardent, passionate, jealous arms of God. How great You are, My Father, to reach out to me with Your compassion, grace, and palpable love!

I found my answer.

The first step: I kept reading verses containing the word "shield."

"Blessed are you, O Israel! [...] a people saved by the LORD [...] He is your shield and helper and your glorious sword" (Deuteronomy 33:29).

The second step: During our *God Chicks* Bible study, our outreach director spoke on Ephesians, chapter six, and the armor of God, as it says: "Therefore put on the full armor of God, so that when the day of evil comes, you may be able to stand your ground, and after you have done everything, to stand. Stand firm then" (Ephesians 6:12-14).

The third step: That same morning, two friends in the study who didn't know I needed to hear this shared these verses:

"Do not be afraid, [...] I am your shield, your very great reward" (Genesis 15:1).

"The LORD will fight for you; you need only to be still" (Exodus 14:14).

I came to a new realization: sometimes warfare is simply standing. But where are we to stand? I don't usually get visions or dreams, but sudden understanding comes into my mind and heart. I remembered Roman generals always led a victory procession into Rome with those they had captured in the parade.

Second Corinthians 2:14 (NET) opened to me: "Thanks be to God who always leads us in triumphal procession in Christ," coupled with Ephesians 4:8, "When he ascended on high, he led captives in his train and gave gifts to men." I don't get visions or dreams, but sudden understanding comes into my mind and heart. The captives Jesus led, including me, including you, are not the conquered but the rescued and ransomed. Aha! I stand on the steps of the throne of God, alongside the victor, Jesus, who holds His shield and sword...

Wait a minute! Christ holds His sword in His left hand, so if He is my shield and glorious sword, that means I am on Jesus's left side, sheltered behind *His* shield! If I am on His left, and He is at the right hand of God, then the Father is on my left side, and I stand sheltered between them both.

The fourth step: That same week, I house-sat for some friends of mine for four days to help their home look "lived in" while they were away. Sitting on their front porch that Sunday morning, my Bible fell open to Song of Songs for my devotional reading, a place I never go for inspiration, but there it was, my Bible flipped open on my lap to Song of Songs 3:11: "Come out you daughters of Zion, and look at King Solomon wearing the crown, the crown with which his mother crowned him on the day of his wedding, the day his heart rejoiced" (Song of Songs 3:11).

And then my eye crossed the page to 4:7: "All beautiful you are, my darling; there is no flaw in you" (Song of Songs 4:7).

I know Song of Songs can be seen as a metaphor for the love God has for us, the bride of Christ, the church (not the institution, but the individuals who comprise the church), so I think the "extrapolation" God gave me is not heretical. In my spirit, I sensed the Holy Spirit telling me (and you, too!) that the Father put a crown on Jesus the day I (and you) came to salvation and became His, our "wedding" day with Him, and on that day, Jesus's heart rejoiced. He sees us as absolutely ravishing, with no flaw at all, thanks to His righteousness, which robes us. I further sensed that my place is standing on the steps of the throne at Jesus's left side, His shield in His left hand (that's His faithfulness) covering and shielding me (you) and His right hand (His promises) fighting the battle for me (and for you). The chains of my captivity to the effects of betrayal, fear, and anger are lying shattered on the steps of the throne of God as a trophy of Jesus's victory in my life when I took Him as my Savior and He took me as His own beloved.

I am a trophy of Jesus's triumph. I am a *trophy bride*; I am *free* (no matter what is going on in my life), and I am ecstatic to be in His embrace as He lifts me upon His shoulder and shows the hosts of heaven, "This is one I have set my love upon!" If you are a man reading this, consider yourself a *trophy son*. I can see Jesus standing before the Father's throne in heaven as each one of us, His children by choice, one day cross over to heaven: "Look, Father, here comes _____! Here he/she comes, Gabriel, so blow that trumpet! Angels, start the singing so _____ and I can dance!"

He rejoices in you, His trophy bride or son, the one whose salvation is a crown upon His head! In the middle of the battle, even if you feel you are sitting in the smoking ashes of your hopes, dreams, health, relationships, security, future, rejoice in the truth that Jesus takes joy in you! Joy in whose you are and where you stand!

Read this passage from Isaiah aloud to tell yourself and the enemy of your soul the truth:

I delight greatly in the Lord; my soul rejoices in my God. For he has clothed me with garments of salvation and arrayed me in a robe of his righteousness, [...] as a bride adorns herself with her jewels.

[...] you will be called by a new name that the mouth of the Lord will bestow. You will be a crown of splendor in the Lord's hand, a royal diadem in the hand of your God. No longer will they call you Deserted, or name your land Desolate. But you will be called Hephzibah, and your land Beulah; for the Lord will take delight in you, and your land will be married. As a young man marries a young woman, so will your Builder marry you; as a bridegroom rejoices over his bride, so will your God rejoice over you.

Isaiah 61:10–62:2-5

Take few moments to pray silently, writing down whatever has held you captive and the battle you face today. Then find whatever you can to represent a shield, whether a book, a magazine, or a pan lid, put on your favorite worship song with whatever means you have to play it, and, silly as this may sound or look to anyone else around you, dance in joy with your Bridegroom,

Jesus. You are a cherished trophy bride, clothed in garments of triumph, lifted in His hands, a glorious crown upon the head of Jesus!

A "but" to pray: Father God, is it really true that You love me this much? Maybe my eyes are on so many people and circumstances down here that I have a hard time seeing You through all the clutter. Are You really this near? I may have a hard time "getting over myself" today, but You are inviting me into a deeper relationship with You, so whether I feel too old or too mature or too sophisticated, today I choose to outrageously raise up my _____

_____ as Your son/bride and sing my favorite song, __

_____,

and believe You're enjoying my unabashed simple love. Yes, show me Your love today in ways I can really get hold of and help me believe it without going through a wilderness. In Jesus's name, amen. Holy Spirit, I'm listening.

How Deeply I'm Known

How intimately our Father knows us! And oh, how He surprises me on a regular basis. Just when you think you have God's intentions tracked and figured out...

Meeting Jessica on "A" Mountain, meeting my dear friend Jann "coincidentally" at the zoo, and meeting Pastor Brian in the kitchen of their house after meeting his wife Jessica on the street after God nudged me to turn around and go down the hill, meeting the man I'd marry after my subscription had expired on a Christian dating site, God connecting me with a writing job after I posted a king-size bed for sale on Facebook...All these "coincidences" certainly were not accidents but meetings planned by God's loving, gracious hand and heart.

Three times in as many days, the person ahead of us in the drive-through line at fast-food restaurants paid for our meal. And last night, in my sleep, I kept hearing, "Isaiah 54:10." When I awoke, I looked up the verse, and there was God again, reaffirming that He loves me, cares about me, wants, wills, and plans the best for me.

> "Though the mountains be shaken and the hills be removed, yet my unfailing love for you will not be shaken nor my covenant of peace be removed," says the Lord, who has compassion on you.
>
> Isaiah 54:10

He's positioned me to carry His word and love for someone else, and what an "energy drink" that is for me to be part of what God Almighty is doing! But to experience Him doing that for me—how humbling, how powerful, what a profound sense of His loving and knowing and being more than able!

"Now this is what the LORD says—he who created you, O Jacob, he who formed you, O Israel: 'Fear not, for I have redeemed you; I have summoned you by name; you are mine'" (Isaiah 43:1).

"I am the good shepherd; I know my sheep, and my sheep know me" (John 10:14).

Oh, to be known by the Creator of the universe—to be called *His*! Treasured, cherished, known!

I recall the time I couldn't afford to splurge on a new dress, but on April 14, after a doctor's appointment, I went to a local thrift store chain and found a spectacular ruddy crimson, gauzy, ankle-length dress embroidered with gold thread and gold sequins for—drum roll please—$6.99. I wore it the next weekend while I presented the Sunday morning devotional message at a women's retreat, testimony to the truth that our Father knows us uniquely as individuals and *cares passionately* about us, uniquely as individuals, as His one-in-a-billion beloved child. That dress restored broken hearts! Thank You, thank You again, Father!

> For you created my inmost being; you knit me together in my mother's womb. I praise you because I am fearfully and wonderfully made; your works are wonderful, I know that full well. My frame was not hidden from you when I was made in the secret place, when I was woven together in the depths of the earth. Your eyes saw my unformed body; all the days ordained for me were written in your book before one of them came to be. How precious to me are your thoughts, God! How vast is the sum of them! Were I to count them, they would outnumber the grains of sand—when I awake, I am still with you.
>
> Psalm 139:13-18

The Israelites took twelve stones from the middle of the Jordan River as they crossed and built an altar on the other side to testify to all of the good things God had done, all of the mighty miracles He'd done for them to free them from slavery in Egypt and bring them safely, fed and clothed, to their promised land forty years later. Writing out a prayer request and recording the answers is like stacking up an altar of "rocks of remembrance": We all need to remember the good things God has done for us, the times He intervened, the blessings He gave, so we don't forget His goodness and faithfulness.

> When all the nation had finished passing over the Jordan, the LORD said to Joshua, "Take twelve men from the people, from each tribe a man, and command them, saying, 'Take twelve stones from here out of the midst of the Jordan, from the very place where the priests' feet stood firmly, and bring them over with you and lay them down in the place where you lodge tonight.'" Then Joshua called the twelve men from the people of Israel, whom he had appointed, a man from each tribe. And Joshua said to them, "Pass on before the ark of the Lord your God into the midst of the Jordan, and take up each of you a stone upon his shoulder, according to the number of the

tribes of the people of Israel, that this may be a sign among you. When your children ask in time to come, 'What do those stones mean to you?' then you shall tell them that the waters of the Jordan were cut off before the ark of the covenant of the Lord. When it passed over the Jordan, the waters of the Jordan were cut off. So these stones shall be to the people of Israel a memorial forever."

Joshua 4:1-7 (ESV)

God showed up for me the very next week at the fountain at the rainforest trail at the zoo where I worked as I was waiting for a very late high school tour group to show up for their tour. Many people passed me heading up the trail, but one woman with her husband stopped and turned to me, startled, and called, "Rose... Mary...Rose?" It had been fourteen years since I'd seen her, but I immediately recognized Jan from my former church. She had moved out of town and lived about a hundred miles to the north now. What an amazed and joyful reunion! We had a wonderful time, reconnecting and praying right there in the middle of traffic, and, to top it off, she and her husband were great friends of the brother of the counselor I was seeing, who lives in the same town they do.

What are the odds of such a random meeting? Spot on 100 percent when Jesus is at work loving and knowing me. What does this mean for you? He knows you, truly knows you, too, and is already at work to meet your deepest heart needs with His ruthless, relentless, mighty, able, and more-than-willing love.

Yes, I believe in miracles...

A "but" to pray: Oh Father, You know me intimately! I may feel nobody understands me or even sees me, *but* You _____.
You truly do put people in my life to meet my needs and speak into my life. Wow, thank You! Right now, Holy Spirit, remind me of times and ways God has demonstrated His love for me. I write them down here as "stones of remembrance":

_____
_____
_____.

Thank you, faithful Father God, for bringing me through these waters to a place, by faith, of blessing. In Jesus's name, amen. Holy Spirit, I'm listening.

_____

What Price Conformity?

I used to read the verse, "And we, who with unveiled faces all reflect the Lord's glory, are being transformed into his likeness with ever-increasing glory which comes from the Lord, who is the Spirit" (2 Corinthians 3:18), and other verses like it that talk about being like Christ, and I'd think, *Oh, yes, God, that's what I want to be!*

Preparing the weekly Sunday school lesson for the elementary-age children in our small church one week, I admit I was shocked to learn that the word for "conform" in this passage is the same word used for striking a coin blank to produce an image on the coin. Ouch, and here's why! From the U.S. Mint website:

> But all blanks need to be prepared before they can be minted.
> First, the blanks are heated in an annealing furnace to soften the metal. Then, they are

run through a washer and dryer. This makes the blanks nice and shiny! Next is upsetting: It's not the bad blanks but the good ones that are upset. Why is that? Because upsetting is the next step in the process. A machine, called an upsetting mill, raises a rim around the edge of the blank. If you run your fingers around a coin, you can feel this tiny raised edge! At this point, the round piece of metal is still a blank. This makes sense—it doesn't yet have the design and lettering that make it a coin. The process of adding the design items is called striking. The upset blanks go through the coining press. All at once, this machine strikes the pictures, amount, and mottoes onto both sides of the blank. The pressure of striking is different for each series and denomination, but pressures somewhere between 50 and 200 tons per square inch are used on modern presses. Now it's a genuine United States coin![4]

Oh, ouch again! Coins usually bore the image of the ruler of the realm. So do we as sons and daughters of God, heirs of Christ Jesus. I realize, though, being conformed to the image of Christ is much more arduous than stamping a heart-shaped eraser in Play-Doh! If I'm truly conformed, I won't look like the "blank" I began as. It doesn't have to hurt if I am as malleable as gold— or better yet, Play-Doh—and as ductile as aluminum!

> As was the earthly man, so are those who are of the earth; and as is the heavenly man, so also are those who are of heaven. And just as we have borne the image of the earthly man, so shall we bear the image of the heavenly man.
>
> 1 Corinthians 15:48-49

"For those God foreknew he also predestined to be conformed to the image of his Son, that he might be the firstborn among many brothers and sisters" (Romans 8:29).

Do I? Do I really want to be the one who smiles and does my best in a less-than-rewarding job, greets my surly boss with a cheerful attitude, sits next to the homeless man who hasn't had a bath in who knows how long, sees beauty in a heavily tattooed and pierced young woman with strangely colored hair? Can I look beyond the sin to see the wounding in the sinner and forgive? Is that what I really want, because that's the reality of being like Jesus: love that never turns away, never gives up! Love that "bears all things, believes all things, hopes all things, endures all things" (1 Corinthians 13:7, ESV).

The trick is to discern true love from codependence and enabling, discern occasional conflicts from chronic issues and true disorders, an angry outburst from abuse, and to know what real love looks like. Sometimes love is tough; love needs to be tough and take a stand for truth, personal dignity, and safety. Sometimes, though, love needs to bend and surrender its "right" to be right for the sake of the right relationship.

Oh, God, truly give me wisdom and understanding! Let me receive what Paul prayed for the believers in Philippi:

> God can testify how I long for all of you with the affection of Christ Jesus. And this is my prayer: that your love may abound more and more in knowledge and depth of insight, so that you may be able to discern what is best and may be pure and blameless for the day of Christ, filled with the fruit of righteousness that comes through Jesus Christ—to the glory and praise of God.
>
> Philippians 1:8-11

Do you sometimes cry out, "God, why don't You... why aren't You...?" I do, but then I realize my deeper question should be, "God, why do You *bother* to love me? Why *do* You, what is it that drives You to love me still in the face of my anger, unbelief, my accusations, complaints, my apathy?"

My real question should be why Jesus had to die to prove God's love for me and why Jesus dying isn't proof enough. Why did it require that? Does God like blood, or, I wonder, is it because our sixth love language, the one we all understand, the one we hold out for and *demand* as proof of love, is sacrifice? Jesus, You gave Your own life for ours. That we understand—maybe.

And even then, we don't believe God loves us! What stubborn, self-preserving pride camouflaged as inferiority and worthlessness drives us to deny such love is possible for us because we need it?

Oh, my recognition of the extravagant, unjustified, unrelenting love of God, and then of the honor He gives me in allowing Him to make me more like Jesus! I'll have to risk people thinking I'm "weird" when I pray for others in public or a "soft touch" when I give something I needed to help someone with a greater need. I'm sure I looked strange the day I stood in the doorway of the women's restroom in a large hotel, sharing God's love with the employee cleaning the restroom and, oh how my heart danced, leading him to ask Jesus into his life as Lord and Savior. For that result, who cares what I looked like? I hope I looked like Jesus! My tears come, too, from knowing that I have been unknowingly enabling in myself—that I had to recognize the lies I had held onto about myself and my value as a human being and child of God, lies that had kept me from being loved and loving unrelentingly—to finally *get it in my gut* that *God is love*, pure and unceasing love.

This conforming business takes me out of my comfort zone. Sometimes I actually have to speak to people about the love of God. Yes, I need to "let my light shine," but sometimes I need to tell them why I'm serving, giving, going the extra mile, making a "fool" of myself in public. "Not everyone has your boldness, Rose," a friend observed, but I countered with, "But everyone knows how much Jesus loves them and can tell their own story of how God pursued them and won them!" If I intend to live as Jesus lived, I need to point others to God's kingdom and love for them by every means possible. Rather than resent God for the pain of being reshaped like Jesus, I now want to press into the truth that Jesus wants to conform me to His likeness out of love.

Jesus was *not* a doormat, even though He did endure scorn, anger, and callous indifference. What He's after is my identity; I realize my identity and value comes from who God sees me to be, accepting that now I have a calling, and then freely encouraging, supporting, and guiding others in my family, friendships, work, church, school, and community to come to *His* unending love as we resemble Jesus in words, thoughts, attitudes, and actions.

> So Christ himself gave the apostles, the prophets, the evangelists, the pastors and teachers, to equip his people for works of service, so that the body of Christ may be built up until we all reach unity in the faith and in the knowledge of the Son of God and become mature, attaining to the whole measure of the fullness of Christ. Then we will no longer be infants, tossed back and forth by the waves, and blown here and there by every wind of teaching and by the cunning and craftiness of people in their deceitful scheming. Instead, speaking the truth in love, we will grow to become in every respect the mature body of him who is the head, that is, Christ. From him the whole body, joined and held together by every supporting ligament, grows and builds itself up in love, as each part does its work.
>
> Ephesians 4:11-16

"God demonstrates his own love for us in this: While we were still sinners, Christ died for us" (Romans 5:8).

A "but" to pray: God, *Abba*, Father, Daddy, maybe not in my mind but in my heart, I have denied Your love

and Your purposes for me over and over again because
_____, *but* I lay that down in
the face of Your relentless love, and I say to You: now
remold me to look like You! Even if You have to ask me
to _____, I will be
bendable, moldable, to clearly carry Your image. What
kind of love can this be that loves me in the face of
my indifference, again and again and again, loves me
enough to not let me stay in my broken, weak, "blank"
state? Conform me to You, not to my culture or other
people's expectations. I don't want to be indifferent
to You or indifferent to or afraid of the people around
me. You want to work through me! Maybe I'm still too
scared to truly want it through me, but because You love
me, I am willing to love _____
and to show it by _____
to _____. Give me wisdom in knowing what
love looks like and joy along the way so I can persist
and pursue and carry Your likeness in me. Show me the
truth, Holy Spirit, and make me a "coin of the realm,"
Jesus. In Jesus's name, amen. Holy Spirit, I'm listening.

DAY 10

I Need A Bigger Pot: Enlarge My Heart and Prayers

Funny how God invades my quiet times and turns my thoughts upside down and inside out!

Yesterday I saw horrendous photos of children—and I mean toddlers—being shot in the head by terrorists, children's bodies lying in rows as hooded men stood over them. This morning I'm reading Psalm 143 and reciting the verses I have memorized, "Save me from my enemies, for I hide myself in you..." and I stop short. This morning, my prayer isn't about me; it isn't meant to be just about the adversary I face in my own life; this morning, the Holy Spirit is enlarging both my heart and my prayers to reach across the world.

Haven't I encouraged other people to do this very thing? On the World Day of Prayer in 2007, I gave a message entitled, "I Need a Bigger Pot" at another church, encouraging the folks assembled to "un-bonsai" their prayer life by taking prayer out of the "my world, my needs" pot, letting their roots and branches grow to un-stunt the growth in the oaks of righteousness they were called to be.

In a split second (God moves at the speed of under-standing, which is sometimes faster than the speed of light), I thought of the prayer of Jabez in 1 Chronicles 4:9-10 and the impact Dr. Bruce Wilkinson's' book by the same title had on me personally and on millions of oth-ers back in 2000 when it hit and flew out of bookstores.

> Jabez was more honorable than his brothers. His mother had named him Jabez, saying, "I gave birth to him in pain." Jabez cried out to the God of Israel, "Oh, that you would bless me and enlarge my territory! Let your hand be with me, and keep me from harm so that I will be free from pain." And God granted his request.
>
> 1 Chronicles 4:9-10

The subtitle of that book was "Breaking Free to the Blessed Life." Oh, my righteous Father, do I think the line about enlarging my territory means "give me more goodness in my life"? Give me influence over more people, in more places, and raise me up to greater accolades and affirmation? No. What prompted me to "un-bonsai" my prayers was a tap on my heart from God one morning as I was unhappily observing the sun-damaged wrinkles on my face. God's spirit quietly reminded me of a Phoenix policeman, Jason Schechterle, whose cruiser crashed into another car on a high-speed chase and erupted in flames. The officer was burned over much of his body, including his face. Even reconstructive surgery left him terribly disfigured, and I was concerned about crow's feet! I repented and immediately prayed for Jason and for other burn victims.

Do I realize that today across the world from my cozy chair, millions of people need healing, a job, a safe place to live, deliverance from human trafficking, salvation for their children? Do I realize that 262 innocent children desperately need to break free of their ungodly, unholy terrorist captors? How often I think of my grandchildren. Do I ever think of children who aren't of my own flesh and blood? Did my heart break yesterday for them? Better question: Did I enlarge the territory of my heart? Did my heart-rent prayers go up for them? *Did I let You, Jesus, enlarge my heart and the breadth and reach and potential of my prayers?*

Read that passage again with God's eyes, with Jesus's heart, with the Holy Spirit's call to you to get down on the floor and pray Psalm 143 *for* your brothers and sisters in more than harm's way. Lift them to the Father. Defend them with the blood of Jesus. Call for some angels to listen up to Psalm 103:20: "Praise the LORD, you his angels, you mighty ones who do his bidding, who obey his word" and give them some Word to take to protect innocent lives.

Read it again, or for the first time, couple it with your desire for God to "enlarge your territory," and extend your heart and your passionate prayers for the persecuted church, dying innocent children, mothers and fathers watching their flesh and blood shot and beheaded. *Does that enlarge your territory?* How does that impact your prayer, "Oh, that you would bless me...and keep me from harm"?

How can I pray that for myself without praying it for that toddler who had six rifles aimed at her precious little head? Can you hear the words of Jesus today in a new way, in a larger territory? What do you hear in His words?

> "For I was hungry and you gave me something to eat, I was thirsty and you gave me something to drink, I was a stranger and you invited me in, I needed clothes and you clothed me, I was sick and you looked after me, I was in prison and you came to visit me."
> Then the righteous will answer him, "Lord, when did we see you hungry and feed you,

or thirsty and give you something to drink?
When did we see you a stranger and invite
you in, or needing clothes and clothe you?
When did we see you sick or in prison and go
to visit you?"
The King will reply, "Truly I tell you, whatever
you did for one of the least of these brothers
and sisters of mine, you did for me."

Matthew 25:35-4

What do you hear Paul speaking to you?

"Carry each other's burdens, and in this way you will
fulfill the law of Christ" (Galatians 6:2).

Is there something, someone you could pick up and
carry in your prayers today?

"And God granted his request." If God sent a yes to
Jabez, won't He send a yes to your passionate prayer?
Don't you think He's waiting for you to ask Him to move
in a way that will show the world His majesty, His holiness, His love, His righteousness, His power? Don't you
think they are waiting for prayers from their brothers
and sisters to join with their own and set captives free?

I'd love for this to reach maybe a million people today: so passionate is my cry to see God move to end this
horrendous, treacherous abomination by *His power in
His way for His glory.* Maybe only one person will read
this. Maybe only one more person will pray. If that per-

son is you, and if you have no idea how to begin, below are Psalm 143 and 144 for you to read out loud. Put their "names" into this word, launch it, and believe with me that:

> As the rain and the snow come down from heaven and do not return to it without watering the earth and making it bud and flourish, so that it yields seed for the sower and bread for the eater, so is my word that goes out from my mouth: it will not return to me empty, but will accomplish what I desire and achieve the purpose for which I sent it.
>
> Isaiah 55:10-11

A "but" to pray today: Lord, Your children all over the world are in peril, literally for their lives, *but You, O God,* promise to hear me when I pray, and I ask You to enlarge my territory, so I pray for them _____ _____ _____. Open my heart and mind to sense, see, and know their needs and feel their hearts _____. I confess my prayers don't often go beyond the boundaries of my personal concerns, *but* I want a bigger heart. Feel free to open my eyes when I hear news stories, read articles online, or see headlines, and prompt me to pray. In Jesus's name, amen, and I pray Your Word now for every child and

every helpless, innocent person in harm's way. Holy
Spirit, I'm listening. "_____
_____." And now, in faith, I declare
Your Word over them:

A psalm of David.

LORD, hear my prayer,
listen to my cry for mercy;
in your faithfulness and righteousness
come to my relief.
Do not bring your servant into judgment,
for no one living is righteous before you.
The enemy pursues me,
he crushes me to the ground;
he makes me dwell in the darkness
like those long dead.
Let the morning bring me word of your un-
    failing love,
for I have put my trust in you.
Show me the way I should go,
for to you I entrust my life.
Rescue me from my enemies, LORD,
for I hide myself in you.

Psalm 143

Praise be to the LORD my Rock,
who trains my hands for war,
my fingers for battle.
He is my loving God and my fortress,
my stronghold and my deliverer,
my shield, in whom I take refuge,
who subdues peoples under me.
LORD, what are human beings that you care
  for them,
mere mortals that you think of them?
They are like a breath;
their days are like a fleeting shadow.
Part your heavens, LORD, and come down;
touch the mountains, so that they smoke.
Send forth lightning and scatter the enemy;
shoot your arrows and rout them.
Reach down your hand from on high;
deliver me and rescue me
from the mighty waters,
from the hands of foreigners
whose mouths are full of lies,
whose right hands are deceitful.
I will sing a new song to you, my God;
on the ten-stringed lyre I will make music to
  you,
to the One who gives victory to kings,
who delivers his servant David.

From the deadly sword deliver me;
rescue me from the hands of foreigners
whose mouths are full of lies,
whose right hands are deceitful.
Then our sons in their youth
will be like well-nurtured plants,
and our daughters will be like pillars
carved to adorn a palace.
Our barns will be filled
with every kind of provision.
Our sheep will increase by thousands,
by tens of thousands in our fields;
our oxen will draw heavy loads.
There will be no breaching of walls,
no going into captivity,
no cry of distress in our streets.
Blessed is the people of whom this is true;
blessed is the people whose God is the LORD.

                                    Psalm 144

Amen and victorious amen!

May I Have This Dance?

Early on a Sunday morning, I gave Jesus an invitation: "Do what will bring You joy, Jesus. Come and dance in my life! Do what will delight You in my life today!"

In the middle of praying, reading the Bible, and singing praise songs, I felt the urge to text a friend, Todd, who plays bass guitar on a worship team. "No, you shouldn't interrupt the flow of worship," I told myself. "Pay attention to the Holy Spirit!" But against my better religious judgment, I went to my phone and sent the text saying I was dancing with Jesus to "Praise to the Lord, the Almighty" on the worship CD of the praise band he played in and prayed Jesus would dance in joyous delight that morning at church through Todd and his team. Bear in mind that I hadn't contacted this friend in over four months when what I wrote happened.

I returned to my singing, and sure enough, I felt somehow that I'd missed the moment and lost the flow, spiritually speaking. I "boarded" another train of thought in my prayer journal until a jingle from my phone announced I had a text message. It was Todd! He texted something that stopped me in mid-journaling: "Your timing is impeccable. I'm preparing to play all three services at Bel Air this morning for the first time in a couple of months. Thanks so much!"

Jesus, *You* did it! *You* were leading me in a dance of blessing in Todd's life, and I never suspected I was dancing with You when I texted him! My prayer journal page morphed into a drawing of a wild series of footsteps punctuated by the words in capital letters: "Dance all over me, Jesus! Dance all over my life! In every place Your feet dance, there lives and resides and rules and reigns Your *glory!*"

Oh, Lord, never let me be so "religious" and inflexible in my "religious duty" that I miss the blessings You want to pour out to me and through me and for me!

Woe to you, teachers of the law and Pharisees, you hypocrites! You give a tenth of your spices—mint, dill and cumin. But you have neglected the more important matters of the law—justice, mercy and faithfulness. You should have practiced the latter, without neglecting the former. You blind guides! You strain out a gnat but swallow a camel. Woe to you, teachers of the law and Pharisees, you hypocrites! You clean the outside of the cup and dish, but inside they are full of greed and self-indulgence. Blind Pharisee! First clean the inside of the cup and dish, and then the outside also will be clean. Woe to you, teachers of the law and Pharisees, you hypocrites! You are like whitewashed tombs, which look beautiful on the outside but on the inside are full of the bones of the dead and everything unclean. In the same way, on the outside you appear to people as righteous but on the inside you are full of hypocrisy and wickedness.

Matthew 23:23-28

"Do not neglect to do good and to share what you have, for such sacrifices are pleasing to God" (Hebrews 13:16, ESV).

Take center stage, Jesus! Zephaniah 3:17 reads: "The LORD your God is with you, he is mighty to save. He will take great delight in you, he will quiet you with his love, he will rejoice over you with singing." The Hebrew word for "rejoice" in this verse implies mirth, gladness, and twirling dance.

Do I ever realize, truly get in my gut, that God rejoices over His children, and I am one of them? Can I envision the great "I AM" giddy with delight when we let Him enter our lives and direct our feet or our texting fingers? I have a strong hunch that Jesus wants to dance with me and in my life much more frequently than I extend the invitation to Him, that my God is much less "religious" than I think—at the very least, less concerned about form and tradition and much more intimate and joyful than we ascribe to Him—and much more the passionately loving Father who genuinely cherishes His kids. I need to give Him more freedom to be Himself in my life for His own pleasure.

"As a young man marries a young woman, so will your Builder marry you; as a bridegroom rejoices over his bride, so will your God rejoice over you" (Isaiah 62:5).

Radical, I know, when we also have to hold in our consciousness at the same time how truly holy and set apart God is. I think my limited pound of brain tissue can only think of Him in one frame of reference at a time, so I've decided I need to be more intentional about giving Jesus center stage on the dance floor in my devotional time. I don't want to become so familiar that I lose sight of His holiness, but I don't want to become so "religious" that I deprive my Creator of His deepest joy. Maybe that's what Jesus had in mind when He told His disciples we have to come to Him as little children.

I loved to see my earthly father grin at me. What a grin I want to see some day on the face of my heavenly Father when I take that running leap into His lap and let Him twirl over me and with me "for real."

I love this song "We Will Dance" from Vineyard Music:

> Sing a song of celebration, lift up a shout of
>   praise
> For the Bridegroom will come, the glorious
>   One
> And oh, we will look on His face
> We'll go, to a much better place
> Dance with all your might, lift up your hands
>   and clap for joy
> The time's drawing near, when He will appear
> And oh, we'll stand by His side
> A strong, pure, spotless bride
> We will dance on the streets that are golden
> The glorious bride and the great Son of Man
> From every tongue and tribe and nation
> Will join, in the song of the Lamb.[5]

In the meantime, Jesus, yes, You may certainly have this dance! You have impeccable timing, and Your footwork in connecting and blessing would win first place in *Dancing with the Stars.* Come to think of it, You probably do dance with the stars!

A "but" to pray: Sometimes, Jesus, I keep You at such a holy distance that I know I don't allow You to enjoy my relationship with You. It's hard to think of You, my God, rejoicing over me with singing, *but* today I choose to let you _____

_____ in and over and through my life and guide my steps every day. Interrupt my agenda and routine wherever and however You desire if there's a blessing I can pass along to someone else today, and I know it will bless me on the rebound when You dance in love in someone else's life, too. How can I make my life and choices into a "line dance" with You today? I won't limit You, Father! In Jesus's name, amen. Holy Spirit, I'm listening.

Roller Coaster Mama

Somewhere between the floor falling away and my body spinning in 360-degree loops as if I were a towel in a clothes dryer, I heard God say, "This is like your life, isn't it?" I had to agree. My father's death from Alzheimer's, followed in rapid succession by my aunt dying one month later of the same disease, my mother's unexpected cancer surgery, and our sudden move across the country bore an uncanny emotional resemblance to the ride I was whirling through. My thoughts flashed back thirty years to the night my fiancé and I were riding the Wild Mouse, a short, jarring little roller coaster at a local amusement park. The ride operator, a friend of my fiancé, kept sending us around the ride again and again. Then it was funny. "But God," I acknowledged, "now it isn't funny."

Instantly I realized it wasn't these major problems, though, keeping me in a constant state of turmoil; it was my reaction to the smaller, daily stresses in my life. I cringed in double conviction, knowing that for a Christian, how I handle stress impacts my discipleship and my witness as well as my body. I took a deep breath as we plunged toward the ground on the aptly named Mind Eraser. Hope filled my mind as breath filled my lungs. I already knew how to manage the stress of riding real roller coasters. Could these same skills apply, as God's question to me seemed to suggest, to coping with stress in everyday life?

Learning to handle thrill rides was essential for me because our younger son Ethan wanted to become a roller coaster designer, and he was serious about it. That meant we rode a lot of roller coasters. The problem, though, was that age, motion sickness, neck problems, and, I admit it, fear displaced my joy in riding roller coasters long before Ethan was born. I sincerely want to participate in what means so much to my child, so I have been forced to look for personal "survival skills" to help me endure these stresses with peace instead of panic.

A few principles that help me manage my stress on roller coasters have proved to be effective with stress in everyday life, too, and I firmly believe they can reduce the negative impact stress has on our minds, relationships, and bodies, as well as on the reflection of our faith. In the interests of blog space, I'll quickly summa-

rize what I usually speak for an hour on, hoping you'll
see the connections without lengthy explanation:

Secure yourself in the restraints

God designed restraints to keep us safe and secure through the stresses and curves of life. Like the
ride designers, God has built simplicity into His safety
systems.

"Love the Lord your God with all your heart and with
all your soul and with all your mind and with all your
strength. The second is this: Love your neighbor as
yourself" (Mark 12:30-31).

Did you ever think of this command as a two-point
safety system to protect your life and your relationships? Think for a minute about what your life would
look like if you just "buckled up" with these two dos:
love God and love others. Living outside of love in resentment, anger, judgment, and bitterness is just like
ignoring the seat belt and standing up on a thrill ride:
it sets us up for accidents when stress loops our lives.
Lives and relationships could be saved from injury or
destruction if we keep our words and actions inside the
vehicle of a loving attitude at all times, even when we're
stressed.

Brace your feet or cross your ankles

"When I said, 'My foot is slipping,' your love, O
LORD, supported me. When anxiety was great within

me, your consolation brought joy to my soul" (Psalm 94:18-19).

If I'm riding a suspended roller coaster where there is no floor, to begin with (ah, the Mind Eraser), or if the floor will at some point drop away beneath me (oy, the Medusa), I cross my ankles so my legs don't whip around uncomfortably on the loops and snap turns. Have you noticed how frequently your foot ends up "in your mouth" when you're stressed, or how often your bad attitude "kicks" the person next to you? Pressing into solid support gives us accountability and stability that strengthen self-control, peace, and patience within us. Ideally, family members support each other in stressful times, but sometimes family members cause the corkscrews! I know I've created stress for the people I love. Christians have the supporting "floor" of God's spirit, but we also need a network of people who will love us enough to push back with truth, with kind correction, with encouragement when we need it, and with practical help, too.

Center your focus

"Every good and perfect gift is from above, coming down from the Father of the heavenly lights, who does not change like shifting shadows" (James 1:17).

Focus is one way my approach to thrill rides differs radically from that of my husband and son, who ride coasters with analytical minds and cast-iron stomachs. They enjoy keeping their eyes open to anticipate the next snap, loop, or dive. For me, anticipation produces anxiety, and my eyes looping all over everywhere set my head spinning. To keep my stomach from churning, I focus on one spot directly in front of me, the way a skater focuses when doing spins—even if that spot is my white knuckles gripping the safety bar—or on the tip of my nose if my eyes are closed. Looking steadily into the distance towards the horizon in the direction in which you are moving, looking toward an unchanging spot helps to reconcile the confusing signals, reorient your perception and restore your sense of balance.

"God is good. God is good..." is the spot I center on again and again when my life starts spinning. God's goodness is unchanging, no matter how confusing the signals we're receiving seem to us.

Be mindful of the truth

Much of the stress I feel in any given situation comes from what I'm thinking about. To reduce my stress level on roller coasters, I tell myself positive truths when I ride: "Thrill ride designers do factor in gravity, material strength, and limitations of human anatomy when they design rides. The theme park owners do not want me to be injured or die. They work to prevent this. The biggest drop on this coaster only lasts 2.8 seconds. I can be at peace for 2.8 seconds." Somewhere back in the far corners of my brain, I do understand this, but that knowledge has a hard time influencing my emotions and my stomach unless I choose to think about it. I have to remind myself of the positive truth.

When I'm stressed, most facts that immediately come to mind are negative, but there are always at least one or two points of positive truth I can think about. I may be powerless to control my circumstances, but I always have the power to direct my thoughts.

"To the Jews who had believed him, Jesus said, 'If you hold to my teaching, you are really my disciples. Then you will know the truth, and the truth will set you free'" (John 8:31-32).

Choose your rides carefully

I have learned the secret of being content in any and every situation, whether well fed or hungry, whether living in plenty or in want. I can do everything through Him who gives me strength (Philippians 4:13).

I ride what I think I can reasonably handle. I try to discern when to ride, when not to ride, and how to say "no" without guilt. Sometimes you have no choice. Sickness or disaster or job loss or someone else's bad choice drops me onto a thrill ride I wasn't standing in line for, but I don't have to create thrill rides for myself or my family by trying to reason with a tired two-year-old, proving to my husband that I'm right, walking in the store just to check what's on sale when our budget is tight, or accomplishing one more thing in the five minutes I have before I need to leave for an appointment.

Five simple reminders on my daily checklist. Some days I run out of the house without so much as a "Good morning, God," and on those days, I'm like a toddler below the weight and height limits, cranking my way up to the first drop on "Boy, I Never Saw This Coming: the Sum of All Stressors." And I never even had to stand in line to get aboard! Okay, Holy Spirit, help me remember to sit down with You, "check in with star command," and go through the God's Word checklist before I even get out of bed!

A "but" to pray: God, I'm stressed today over _____, *but* I know You are riding with me. Show me where I need to secure myself _____ _____. Do I need to brace myself with someone who can hold me accountable, or am I missing Your truth somewhere? Did I get myself on a ride I should have never ridden? If I did, Holy Spirit, please show me how to get off with dignity, grace, respect and courtesy _____ _____. Jesus, your limitless love and power give me contentment and strength for every ride, so Lord, let me be a roller coaster mama! I'm sure this week, life will take me on a thrill ride, but with

Your help, I won't panic, hyperventilate, or scream. I'll buckle into love for You and others, even the ones ___

_____ who put me on the roller coasters. I'll press into a supporting floor and brace my feet at the foot of the cross. I'll choose positive truth and center my focus on You. When it is within my power to choose what I get involved in, I will be wise about my choices. When it isn't within my power to choose, I'll trust in Jesus's limitless power to strengthen me, and by faith, I believe I'll even enjoy the ride! In Jesus's name, amen. Holy Spirit, I'm listening.

Do Do What You Need to Do in Me

I'm not the bling, gel manicure, and sequined frou-frou kind of girl. I do like to get dressed up, and I enjoy wearing jewelry and perfume, but I'm just not a "ruffles and matching purse/matching shoes/matching nail polish/matching bling" woman. I'm not even sure I'd feel comfortable doing that if I could afford to (which I can't). I hear from God in analogies, and while I admire other Christian women speakers who get to deliver the "pretty boxes with ribbons and bows" kinds of messages, God never seems to speak to me through glitzy, girlie things. I "hear" Him through tent stakes, roller coasters, and cheeseburgers. Nevertheless, I was surprised this morning by what God used to teach me something: picking up after my dog in the side yard.

All I intended to do in the yard was take advantage of rain-dampened ground to pull pesky spurge, the bane of my gardening, from the backyard. Weeding is unpleasant enough, but as I crouched down, working my way beyond the orange tree, I came to a huge patch of spurge smack in the middle of a field of doggie doo. Aargh! I like dogs, but when our son wanted a pet ten years ago, I voted for a hamster: they only live a couple of years, and they don't shed all over the house. My husband vetoed my vote, asserting, "If we're going to get a pet, it's going to be a dog." Enter our adorable Springer Spaniel puppy Katie.

Flash forward through ten years of me brushing, feeding, medicine giving, ear cleaning, ball throwing, bone cooking, daily walking, hair vacuuming, and doo-doo picking up. Yes, our son used to do some of the walking and picking up, but he moved away to college four years ago. Yes, my husband occasionally cleans up the backyard and walks the two dogs (we now have our older son's dog also), maybe two evenings a week and sometimes on Sunday mornings, and yes, he's the one who works to buy the dog chow and pay the vet bills, but this morning, as usual, I'm the one whose nose is eighteen inches away from the recycled dog chow covering the backyard, and I'm not happy about it.

Two thoughts occurred to me: *We could hire someone to do the yard work, but no, we can't afford it,* and my habitual complaint, *Why does it have to be me picking up the poo? He has time in the evenings to do a little bit if he really cared!*

I'm not the one who wanted a dog! had only briefly, sarcastically flashed through my miffed mind when, on the heels of grumbling, like Katie after a pigeon, came the thought, *Even if you hired someone to pull the weeds and pick up the doo-doo, it wouldn't take care of the real issue. What stinks the most here is not the doo-doo in the yard but the doo-doo in your attitude...*

I knew that idea didn't come from me! God patiently humors me a lot, and I recognized His heart in the thought. Hiring someone to clean the yard would still leave me with doo-doo in my heart, and a stinky attitude is not what God wants for me or what I really want for myself.

"Okay, I've tried the positive thinking thing before," I countered. "Cleaning up the dog poo is a way to show our son I love him because he loves the dog. That gets me through three minutes of picking up, maybe. Jesus, I need You to really get hold of my heart in this." That morning I needed more than just a cheerful veneer because I wanted that change to be lasting. I don't want weekly deposits of resentment in my heart. I want a clean heart more than I want a weed-free, poo-free yard.

God gave me the thought: "Bless your husband as you pick up the poo. Yes, I know you've tried before, but this morning, make it not just words of dry obedience, but truly bless him."

So I did. As I looked up, I saw opportunities all around me for plenty of blessings! I prayed, "I don't like what my hands are in right now, but bless the work of his hands today. He works so hard for us. Give him satisfying work to do with his hands because I know how stressed he feels doing nothing but paperwork. I know I've made some stinky choices he has had to 'pick up.' This doo-doo reminds me that he hangs in there with me when I'm not so pleasant to deal with." I honestly felt a shift in my attitude. God moved through my willing-to-change heart. If I bless his hands as mine are doing something I don't want to do, then this doo-doo can become a springboard (a Springer board?) for God's healing changes in me.

Can you guess what I heard from my husband that evening? "I had a great day today! I actually got to sit in the cockpit and play with the radio. Maybe next week, I'll get a ride to check things out!" God blessed him even as I was praying. Retrospectively, that made the doo-doo duty, while not pleasant, something even better: rewarding. I could almost hear the laughter in heaven. Gosh, God is fun! Why don't I remember that in the middle of my messes? Can you tell what the following two "therefores" are there for?

Therefore I, the prisoner of the Lord, implore you to walk in a manner worthy of the calling with which you have been called, with all humility and gentleness, with patience, showing tolerance for one another in love, being diligent to preserve the unity of the Spirit in the bond of peace.

Ephesians 4:1-3 (NASB)

"Therefore, since Christ suffered in his body, arm yourselves also with the same attitude, because he who has suffered in his body is done with sin" (1 Peter 4:1).

Do all things without grumbling or disputing, that you may be blameless and innocent, children of God without blemish in the midst of a crooked and twisted generation, among whom you shine as lights in the world.

Philippians 2:14-15 (ESV)

Finally, brothers, whatever is true, whatever is honorable, whatever is just, whatever is pure, whatever is lovely, whatever is commendable, if there is any excellence, if there is anything worthy of praise, think about these things. What you have learned and received and heard and seen in me—practice these things, and the God of peace will be with you.

Philippians 4:8-9 (ESV)

"Search me, O God, and know my heart! Try me and know my thoughts! And see if there be any grievous way in me, and lead me in the way everlasting!" (Psalm 139:23-24, ESV)

Has someone else made choices that leave you with doo-doo to deal with?

Please don't hear what I'm *not* saying! I'm not promoting codependent behavior or cleaning up other people's messes and removing the consequences of their poor choices from them. What I am talking about is my heart, your heart: how we handle the fallout of choices other people make that impact our lives in burdensome, frustrating, irritating, even painful ways. Society often tells us the answer is to get rid of the doo-dropping person. Sometimes, and in cases of abuse, that is the safe and appropriate thing to do. For most of the messes we deal with, though, that isn't a good, healthy, or effective solution, and it doesn't deal with the heart issues that are left behind. Sometimes you can't change what you have to deal with or get around it: you just have to pick up the doo-doo. But you can choose your attitude and choose to bless, which can change you as well.

I couldn't get rid of our dog Katie; our son would've been crushed, and I'd have missed her so much, too. Honestly, I do now, even two years after she went to the big kibble bowl in the sky. (Genuinely, I do hope, as the animated kids' movie claiming All Dogs Go to Heaven.) As God revealed to me this morning, though, Katie wasn't the critical issue. It's my heart that matters to Him, and thank God it does! My family and I can work out the cleanup schedule...or I can keep blessing them as Katie's picture on my computer's screensaver drops me reminders!

I share my own flawed humanity here in hope and faith with one of you who needs God's transforming power to turn something stinky in your life into an avenue of blessing this very day and find healing for your heart attitude today. I'm confident no women's ministry director will ever ask me to speak on this topic, so this is the only place you'll hear it!

Maybe one of these days, yet God will give me a message through a pretty box with ribbons, or jewelry, or nail polish?

A "but" to pray: Tender Father, I struggle so with a bad attitude over

_____. I admit: it stinks to other people and to You. I trust You, and I know You will help me, so tell me what I need to change in my thinking

_____.

Father, as much as I want to, I don't have the persistent commitment in myself to change my stinky attitudes, and I admit that sometimes I don't even want to. I'm quick to spot the doo-doo from other people's choices and often blind to the messes in my heart, *but* You are kind enough to both reveal them and set me on the path to healing and peace in my relationships. I don't want to live in denial of what's going on in my life; I want Your sound mind and wholesome, positive attitude in everything and with everyone I deal with, even when those things and people don't change. I give You permission, Holy Spirit, to show me any "stinkin' thinkin'" in my heart and thoughts, and I ask you to replace them with thoughts of ways I can bless _____

_____. *Do* do in me all it takes to transform *me* into an avenue of blessing always. God, You are the Creator and Author of creativity, so I dare to ask You for creativity in my attitudes to create in me a truly clean heart and renew a right spirit within me. I know this is a prayer You've been waiting for me to offer up, so I know You will help me! Thank You, and I look forward to the new ideas, attitudes, and gratitude You'll put into my heart through Your Spirit in my spirit. In Jesus's name, amen! Holy Spirit, I'm listening.

God of My Steps and Missteps

Who would have thought, I mused, that parking at the wrong end of the mall would turn out to be so much fun?

What a morning of mistakes and missteps! They started when I read the wrong appointment card for my hand surgeon and missed a day of work, cutting our dogs' walk short by twenty minutes so I could fly out the door, leap into the car, and speed to what I thought was a 9:00 a.m. appointment. The puzzled look in the receptionist's eyes morphed into a bemused grin of "oh, this poor confused old lady" as she sadly informed me that my appointment wasn't until four that afternoon. Wrinkles from too many hiking trips move younger people to see senility instead of a love for the outdoors in my appearance!

"Oh, crumb!" I chided myself. "I must have read the '4' I wrote as a '9'!" Quickly shrugging off the $72 I had just lost in missed pay, I opted to make the best of the situation and save gas by popping over to the quick-fix jeweler in the nearby mall to get two bent prongs on my engagement ring repaired.

June in Arizona marks the beginning of the season when one is willing to walk from the farthest spot in the parking lot as long as it's under a tree or even a healthy bush offering a spotty patch of shade, so I rejoiced in finding a parking space not only close to a mall entrance, but also beneath a leafy canopy of shade. Imagine my consternation to discover that the store whose entrance I parked near didn't open for another hour! Grumbling at misstep number two, I tramped back to my car and drove around to the northeast side of the mall, where surely the generic mall entrance must be open at 9:00 a.m. And true enough, it was.

Misstep number three: the jewelry repair shop was in the northwest corner of the mall, so I had to walk the entire length of the mall!

"I needed the exercise anyway," I philosophized, still leaning into optimism or at least leaning away from mounting frustration. That meant I had to hike the length of the mall again at 10:00 when my ring was fixed, running the gauntlet of the now-open kiosks that flanked the food court.

"Have you heard of Dead Sea minerals?" a young man called as I attempted to zip by.

"Yes, are you Ahava?" I shot back breezily, hoping to brush him off.

"No, we aren't..." he replied.

Oh, what the heck? I thought, *I might as well get the nails on one hand buffed.* That's fully what, and all, I expected to happen. Twenty minutes later, though, I wonderingly waved goodbye to Avi and Elan after chatting with them a bit, sharing what I recently learned of the meaning of the Hebrew letters *yud, heh, vav, heh* ("the hand of grace, nailed in grace"), Isaiah 53:5: "But he was pierced for our transgressions," and praying for the success of their little stand and for peace in Israel.

Elan was genuinely touched that I would pray for them. Yes, I walked away with a nail care kit, too, but I walked away with an awed joy that Jesus continues to use me, even in my brokenness, to touch other people's lives with His love. After the person you've trusted the most tells you that you are worthless, hearing from Jesus that you are precious enough for Him to speak through rains down worth, dignity, value, and a joy that sets your heart dancing!

I've bumbled and stumbled my way into God's plans and purposes much more frequently than I've intentionally found them through my own efforts: the man who'd lost his wife to Alzheimer's so that I could encourage his heart that her spirit was still intact inside her failing brain, the new dear friend I have when I was asked to choose the name of an advocate off a list of people I didn't know, a woman I met in the parking lot of a church who'd just come out of the prayer chapel and was asking God to show her that he heard her prayer when I walked up and asked, "Is there some way I can pray for you?"

Oh, those blessed missteps that led me to an encounter with God! Abba, can I dare to believe that even a trek through a dark valley is, in fact, a pilgrimage under light I simply can't see, a journey to a victory more beautiful than I can imagine?

Some days—days of mistakes and missteps—my heart dares to trust this is, in fact, the truth I can hang my heart on!

> I will instruct you and teach you in the way you should go; I will counsel you with my loving eye on you. Do not be like the horse or the mule, which have no understanding but must be controlled by bit and bridle or they will not come to you. Many are the woes of the wicked, but the LORD's unfailing love surrounds the one who trusts in him.
>
> Psalm 32:8-10

> The LORD makes firm the steps of the one who delights in him; though he may stumble, he will not fall, for the LORD upholds him with his hand. I was young and now I am old,

yet I have never seen the righteous forsaken or their children begging bread. They are always generous and lend freely; their children will be a blessing. Turn from evil and do good; then you will dwell in the land forever. For the LORD loves the just and will not forsake his faithful ones.

Psalm 37: 23-28

"Who, then, are those who fear the LORD? He will instruct them in the ways they should choose" (Psalm 35:12).

Lead me, O LORD, in your righteousness because of my enemies; make your way straight before me [...] But let all who take refuge in you rejoice; let them ever sing for joy and spread your protection over them, that those who love your name may exult in you. For you bless the righteous, O LORD; you cover him with favor as with a shield.

Psalm 5:8, 11-12 (ESV)

"In their hearts humans plan their course, but the LORD establishes their steps" (Proverbs 16:9).

What an amazing, wonderful, ever-gracious God we love and serve! Who else can take our "bumper car uh-ohs" and turn them into blessings?

A "but" to pray: Lord, I want to walk straight into Your plans and purposes and blessings for me, but some days I find myself going in what seems like circles. Some days, the way I want to go seems blocked. I do get frustrated, *but* maybe, just maybe, You have a different direction for me to take? Maybe You have a blessing along the way when I have to go a different way than I planned? Maybe You're keeping me from something I shouldn't be involved in? Remind me right now of a time when I couldn't go the way I planned, but You brought blessing _____

_____. Sometimes it's hard to hear Your voice, and sometimes I make mistakes that I think are too big for You to handle and correct my course. But, Father, God Almighty, King of Kings and Lord of Lords, You say nothing is too difficult for You, and You promise to cause all things to work together for my good; I give You permission and more, I ask You to *please* teach me and instruct me in the way I should go, and guide me truly with Your eye on me and looking ahead to guide me, so I don't waver or slip off the path of Your blessings. When Your blessing comes, help me recognize it! Is it here now in_____

_____? Thank You, Father, in Jesus's name, amen! Holy Spirit, I'm listening.

God at Arm's Length

I simply can't sit on my hands to worship or want an at-a-distance relationship with God. I have no criticism or judgment of people who feel comfortable in very traditional liturgical churches, and I do, in fact, come from a "call to worship, responsive reading, first-third-and-fifth verses of traditional hymns" faith background, but my deepening intimacy with Jesus puts such a passionate desire to connect with Him into my worship that I can't sit down to sing or fold my hands politely in my lap for fear of upsetting the establishment. Out of town at a conference one weekend, I attended a congregation of the denomination I grew up in. As familiar as it all was and as wonderful as the people were, I couldn't ignore the tugging in my heart to really receive from God and enter into vibrant communion with Him in a powerfully personal way.

When I visit my extended family, I don't stiffly shake their hands and say, "Oh, blessed Aunt Pat, revered Uncle Dean, how fond I am of you." No, I run up to her and to him, wrap him and her in a big hug, and we squeeze each other with laughter and words of affection pouring out.

I cannot keep God at a distance either, and I hope God isn't comfortable with nothing but a stiff, formal relationship with me. After worship in my denominational church that weekend, I discretely got up, left the service, and drove to another church I'd heard of in that small town. It hit me as soon as I walked into the second church, cut loose to get real and a bit wild with Jesus: I want a God who "gets in my face" and "messes with my business." How else can I be changed, challenged to grow, transformed into the *me* God created me to be and the me I desperately want to be if He doesn't get intimately involved in my life? Intimacy is messy, boundary crossing, and comfort-zone rattling. Frankly, I pray that the Lover of my soul loves me enough to not want me to remain less than the best and greatest I'm meant and created to be. I've touched the relentless longing and heard the passionate beat of God's heart for me. Oh, to be loved by a jealous God who desires a vibrant relationship with me!

"Listen, O daughter, consider and give ear. Forget your people and your father's house. The king is en-

thralled by your beauty; honor him, for he is your lord"
(Psalm 45:10-11).

I realize two truths counterpoised: while not everyone feels comfortable with a "wild at heart" God, and
people who've grown up with formal liturgy often find
comfort in liturgy, nevertheless, who would want or
worship a "manageable" God who can be accessed only
by ritual and routine? Some people feel deep rever-
ence in high liturgy, ornate decoration, and vestments
that reflect to them the holiness of God. I can be swept
away in singing old hymns, but I don't object to raising
my hands and swaying a bit if I truly want to exult in
the joy of belonging to Jesus. If God can't shake up my
paradigms, I ask myself, am I trying to keep Him as a
museum piece to be admired but not entered into as a
living, powerful, personal, relational reality?

> Jesus stepped into a boat, crossed over and
> came to his own town. Some men brought to
> him a paralyzed man, lying on a mat. When
> Jesus saw their faith, he said to the man, "Take
> heart, son; your sins are forgiven." At this,
> some of the teachers of the law said to them-
> selves, "This fellow is blaspheming!" Know-
> ing their thoughts, Jesus said, "Why do you
> entertain evil thoughts in your hearts? Which
> is easier: to say, 'Your sins are forgiven,' or to

say, 'Get up and walk'? But I want you to know that the Son of Man has authority on earth to forgive sins." So he said to the paralyzed man, "Get up, take your mat and go home." Then the man got up and went home. When the crowd saw this, they were filled with awe; and they praised God, who had given such authority to man. As Jesus went on from there, he saw a man named Matthew sitting at the tax collector's booth. "Follow me," he told him, and Matthew got up and followed him.

While Jesus was having dinner at Matthew's house, many tax collectors and sinners came and ate with him and his disciples. When the Pharisees saw this, they asked his disciples, "Why does your teacher eat with tax collectors and sinners?" On hearing this, Jesus said, "It is not the healthy who need a doctor, but the sick. But go and learn what this means: 'I desire mercy, not sacrifice.' For I have not come to call the righteous, but sinners."

Then John's disciples came and asked him, "How is it that we and the Pharisees fast often, but your disciples do not fast?" Jesus answered, "How can the guests of the bridegroom mourn while he is with them? The time will come when the bridegroom will be taken from them; then they will fast. No one sews a patch of unshrunk cloth on an old garment, for the patch will pull away from the garment, making the tear worse. Neither do people pour new wine into old wineskins. If they do, the skins will burst; the wine will run out and the wineskins will be ruined. No, they pour new wine into new wineskins, and both are preserved."

Matthew 9:1-17

Jesus entered into the messiness in people's lives. He withdrew to hillsides to be alone with His Father, but He sat down to eat with tax collectors, and He touched women and lepers. He "broke the rules" of tradition to bring the vitally alive presence of God into the sickness and sin and dirt of our world to heal the sick, mend the broken, and raise the dead, and He never wore a gilded cassock or paraded slowly down an aisle to do it.

Then some Pharisees and teachers of the law came to Jesus from Jerusalem and asked, "Why do your disciples break the tradition of the elders? They don't wash their hands before they eat!" Jesus replied, "And why do you break the command of God for the sake of your tradition? For God said, 'Honor your father and mother' and 'Anyone who curses their father or mother is to be put to death.' But you say that if anyone declares that what might have been used to help their father or mother is 'devoted to God,' they are not to 'honor their father or mother' with it. Thus you nullify the word of God for the sake of your tradition. You hypocrites! Isaiah was right when he prophesied about you:'These people honor me with their lips, but their hearts are far from me. They worship me in vain; their teachings are merely human rules.'"

Jesus called the crowd to him and said, "Listen and understand. What goes into someone's mouth does not defile them, but what comes out of their mouth, that is what defiles them."

Then the disciples came to him and asked, "Do you know that the Pharisees were offended when they heard this?" He replied, "Every plant that my heavenly Father has not planted will be pulled up by the roots. Leave them; they are blind guides. If the blind lead the blind, both will fall into a pit."

Peter said, "Explain the parable to us."

"Are you still so dull?" Jesus asked them. "Don't you see that whatever enters the mouth goes into the stomach and then out of the body? But the things that come out of a person's mouth come from the heart, and these defile them. For out of the heart come evil thoughts—murder, adultery, sexual immorality, theft, false testimony, slander. These are what defile a person; but eating with unwashed hands does not defile them."

Matthew 15:1-16

Oh LORD, you have searched me and you know me. You know when I sit and when I rise; you perceive my thoughts from afar [...] you are familiar with all my ways [...] You hem me in behind and before; you have laid your hand upon me. Such knowledge is too wonderful for me, too lofty for me to attain. Where can I go from your Spirit? Where can I flee from your presence?

Psalm 139:1-7

Why would I want to flee from God's presence? This presence is the God who spilled His own blood in agony to secure my relationship with Him forever! Early one Sunday morning, I sat in a chair in the loft of my older son's house, wrapped in a comforter, leaning into the dim light to read the Bible in my quiet time. Suddenly, my six-year-old granddaughter, Elsa, crept up, crawled under the comforter with me, took my small travel Bible in her hands, and began reading from Psalm 27: "One thing I ask of the LORD, this is what I seek: that I may dwell in the house of the LORD all the days of my life, to gaze upon the beauty of the LORD and to seek him in his temple, for in the day of trouble he will keep me safe in his dwelling; he will hide me in the shelter of his ta—"

She stumbled with the word, and I guessed, "Tabernacle?"

"Yes," Elsa replied. "Tabernacle."

"Do you know what a tabernacle is?" I mused.

She nodded her head. "It's the place where God lived."

"The tent where the people worshipped Him in the desert," I added.

"And," she went on, not missing a beat, "I learned in chapel that it's like God's wings. God's wings are soft and strong." Those beautiful blue eyes looked up into mine, and she snuggled closer.

"Grandma, it's like your prayer shawl we hid under the last time you were here."

And what she said next so sincerely, innocently, frankly took my breath away, the Word of God out of the mouth of a child: "Yes, and Grandma, those knots on it are so tight that nobody could untie them!"

The knots on my prayer shawl, my tallit, representing every promise God made to His people, extend to us, so tightly promised that no way will God ever "untie" them!

"Hey, Elsa, you're right, God is tight with us! You and I are 'tight.'" I drew her closer in a fun, wiggling hug. "Do you know what it means to be 'tight' with someone?" She shook her head, and I whispered, "It means nothing can ever come between our love."

Why on earth would I want to keep a "respectful" emotional and liturgical distance from the God who wants to be so "tight" with me that His promises will never fail: He'll never untie them!

So this morning, I figuratively leaped into the arms of the King of Kings, held His hands and danced a little salsa with Him (Wasn't that exactly what we were singing?) and invited Him—no, implored Him—to be "tight" with me, get in my face and mess with my business as much as He wants to and needs to, even when it's uncomfortable, like the ways He's causing me to recognize and face my fear, impatience and submission issues to grow me into everything He wants in me, for me, and through me.

Fair warning: even if I'm holding a hymnal and sitting still next to you to respect the traditions in your worship service some Sunday morning, I'll be dancing on the inside. A little salsa on Sunday is a very good thing, so mess with me, Holy Spirit!

A "but" to pray: Oh, God, really I'd like to hide my issues of _____ from You, *but*, deeper still, I don't want to be held back and crippled by _____, made less than the best You want for me. So I give You permission to get in my face and mess with my business _____ _____. Help me to open my heart wide and lift it to You when I worship, even if lifting my hands high would make people around me feel uncomfortable, even if I'd feel uncomfortable raising my hands when no one else was. I give You permission to flood me with joy in Your love for me, with joy that erupts out of the limits of tradition and what others think is "right and proper" to truly rejoice in who You are and who I am to You. How do You want me to worship You today from the depths of my heart?

_____

_____. Thank You that You want to be real and alive in my life! In Jesus's name, amen. Holy Spirit, I'm listening.

_____

The Sea Glass War

The rocket attack came out of the blue. My husband "Cliff" and I were standing in the long line in front of the auditorium the night of our younger son's final high school chorus concert when our son called on my cell phone to ask if he could borrow some money so a fellow singer who hadn't had dinner could get something to eat before the show. Phone in hand, I turned to Cliff and explained, "Ethan wants to borrow some money to help..." I asked my husband if that would be okay, and he angrily fired off, "He's your son!" Whoa—where did that come from?

Shell-shocked, I couldn't imagine what provoked his angry attack or even what his comment meant. I didn't know we were at war! Our son came out to get the money and told me it was for a good friend from church. "It's for his friend from church, Anna," I related to Cliff, thinking an explanation would help, and he snapped, "Don't tell me that. I don't need to know!" Two rounds fired! This was no accidental friendly fire shooting! Instantly my defensive shields went up. I felt angry and confused, but I couldn't lob any verbal grenades back at my husband because the women's ministry director of our church was standing three people ahead of me. Trapped! I was pinned down, unable to defend myself.

Usually, I'd launch a verbal retaliatory strike or at least set the launch codes and fire later when I had the opportunity. This night, though, I resolved not to return anger for anger. I didn't want to cause a scene in line or ruin the evening, but I also didn't think it would be healthy to let the incident go and pretend this conflict never happened. *I've responded that way too many times in the past, and it only made me resentful,* I recalled as I took a deep breath. What to do? In an unusual step back from the brink of mutual annihilation, I decided to make a hopefully permanent change and quickly resolved to look for a way to deal with the conflict in a way both respectful to my husband and healthy for our relationship. I silently sent a prayer SOS, "Jesus, please tell me how to handle my anger," and held my fire.

I didn't say anything when we got home that night, but the next morning I prayed again to discern a positive way to express my feelings while bringing a healthy resolution to the issue for both my husband and me. At the breakfast table, I calmly told my husband, "I feel your words last night were intentionally hurtful. Would you speak to people at work the way you did to me?"

"No," he said, "but I don't think what I said was hurtful." Inside I was thinking, Oh, come on, but I made a conscious choice and effort to quickly subdue my frustration. "Would you speak to your associates that way?" I repeated. My husband replied that he wouldn't because no one at work would speak to him the way I did. Puzzled because I hadn't said anything nasty to him the night before, but feeling a peace that surely came from God, I replied, "Your comment indicates that you do realize the words were hurtful." I, honestly, simply stated, "I can't think of anything I said last night to merit those hostile words." Did I miss something? And was I speaking in disrespect?

I'd presented my case without becoming defensive. What would happen next? Amazingly my husband's demeanor changed, and he acknowledged that he had been angry and intentionally used those words to drive home the fact. At that point, we were able to identify what had actually angered him, discuss the situation, and come to a healthy resolution.

God turned what could have been explosive and damaging into something healthy. Because it was unexpectedly healing, and because I felt enabled to uncharacteristically say something that maintained my dignity while still respecting my husband, to me, the encounter was profoundly beautiful. Years ago, I wrote an analogy comparing anger to broken glass on a playground, shiny and attractive, but you'd warn your child not to pick it up because, attractive as it looks, broken glass easily cuts anyone who handles it. Anger cuts and wounds relationships. If she or he picked up a piece of broken glass, you'd immediately ask your child to either drop it or carefully hand it to you, so you could take care of it safely and properly. In the analogy, I wrote that the proper thing to do with anger is to hand it to Jesus so that He can dispose of it safely.

After our "chorus line" battle, though, I realized Jesus did more than just dispose of my anger. When I resolved to respect Cliff and our relationship and placed my anger in His hands, Jesus transformed it into something precious that restored rather than destroyed. Shards of broken anger became beautiful like rounded sea glass, a powerful affirmation to keep choosing my resolution. At American Craft Works, I found a description of the process that turns trashed, broken bottles into beautiful sea glass:

> The ocean's saltwater and sand combined with the various tides act like a giant rock tumbler & eventually turn sharp broken glass into beautifully rounded frosted jewels that wash up on the shoreline. [6]

I handed Jesus the broken glass of my anger, and He returned to me, healing communication with my husband, something beautiful to be valued and prized like a sea glass gem. That day I changed my reaction and witnessed a battlefield turning into a beach.

Our feelings are our feelings, but we do well to look deeply within and pray to discern the hurt, disappointment, or expectation unmet that pushed a "hot button." We all have them hidden inside: hurts, slights, fears, and insecurities in childhood that we didn't know how to process in healthy ways then. The longer I go through life, the more broken people I find: people with wounds from an absent or present but controlling and rigidly unloving father, abandonment either emotional or actual from their mother, burying deep inside them the questions, "Will anyone love me for who I am? Do I matter to someone? How can I find the love I need?"

Legitimate needs and questions, but how we express them to others can bring healing or raise up like quills on a porcupine's back, pushing others away with our angry barbs aimed at them personally, rather than expressing the need we have in clear, positive ways others can respond to.

God has much to say about anger:

"A soft answer turns away wrath, but a harsh word stirs up anger" (Proverbs 15:1, ESV).

"A hot-tempered man stirs up strife, but he who is slow to anger quiets contention" (Proverbs 15:18, ESV).

"Good sense makes one slow to anger, and it is his glory to overlook an offense" (Proverbs 19:11, ESV).

> What causes quarrels and what causes fights among you? Is it not this, that your passions are at war within you? You desire and do not have, so you murder. You covet and cannot obtain, so you fight and quarrel. You do not have, because you do not ask.
>
> James 4:1-2 (ESV)

"Whoever is slow to anger is better than the mighty, and he who rules his spirit than he who takes a city" (Proverbs 16:32, ESV).

> Be angry and do not sin; do not let the sun go down on your anger, and give no opportunity to the devil. [...] Let no corrupting talk come out of your mouths, but only such as is good for building up, as fits the occasion, that it may give grace to those who hear. [...] Let all bitterness and wrath and anger and clamor and slander be put away from you, along with all malice. Be kind to one another, ten-

derhearted, forgiving one another, as God in Christ forgave you.

Ephesians 4:26, 29, 31-32 (ESV)

But now you must put them all away: anger, wrath, malice, slander, and obscene talk from your mouth. Do not lie to one another, seeing that you have put off the old self[a] with its practices and have put on the new self, which is being renewed in knowledge after the image of its creator. [...] Put on then, as God's chosen ones, holy and beloved, compassionate hearts, kindness, humility, meekness, and patience, bearing with one another and, if one has a complaint against another, forgiving each other; as the Lord has forgiven you, so you also must forgive.

Colossians 3:8-10, 12-13 (ESV)

Not many of you should become teachers, my brothers, for you know that we who teach will be judged with greater strictness. For we all stumble in many ways. And if anyone does not stumble in what he says, he is a perfect man, able also to bridle his whole body. If we put bits into the mouths of horses so that they obey us, we guide their whole bodies as well. Look at the ships also: though they are so large and are driven by strong winds, they are guided by a very small rudder wherever the will of the pilot directs. So also the tongue is a small member, yet it boasts of great things. How great a forest is set ablaze by such a small fire! And the tongue is a fire, a world of unrighteousness. The tongue is set among our members, staining the whole body, setting on fire the entire course of life, and set on fire by hell. For every kind of beast and bird, of reptile and sea creature, can be tamed and has been tamed by mankind, but no human being can tame the tongue. It is a restless evil, full of deadly poison. With it we bless our Lord and Father, and with it we curse people who are made in the likeness of God. From the same mouth come blessing and cursing. My brothers, these things ought not to be so. Does a spring pour forth from the same opening both fresh and salt water? Can a fig tree, my brothers, bear olives, or a grapevine produce figs? Neither can a salt pond yield fresh water. Who is wise and understanding among you? By his good conduct let him show his works in the meekness of wisdom. But if you have bitter jealousy and selfish ambition in your hearts, do not boast and be false to the truth. This is not the wisdom that comes down from above, but is earthly, unspiritual, demonic. For where jealousy and selfish ambition exist, there will be disorder and every vile practice. But the wisdom from above is first pure, then peaceable, gentle, open to reason, full of mercy and good fruits, impartial and sincere. And a harvest of righteousness is sown in peace by those who make peace.

James 3:1-18 (ESV)

If you have, or have a loved one with, a deeply entrenched chronic anger issue, please seek professional help for both the angry person and the one(s) living with them. It may be rooted in a deep wound from childhood trauma, which needs to be addressed with professional help. All of us can easily speak before we think, and we tend to react rather than respond when someone "pushes our buttons." My prayer for others and me is a cry, hands lifted to God, to help me/us do what we instinctively can't and bring to the light of His healing the hurts that lead us to speak and act harshly. What beautiful gems God can make of us when we give our anger to Him for His understanding, compassionate, and passionate healing. The wonderful truth is that God wants to heal our wounds!

A "but" to pray: Oh, Loving Father, I do feel angry when ______________________________, and when I do, I know my words can wound. You don't condemn me because I have needs and desires, but please help me to see deep inside myself to the root of the emotions that drive me to express my needs and expectations in unhealthy ways. Holy Spirit, I open myself to You now and give You permission to show me things You long to heal ______________________________ ______________________________. People in my life do irritate me, including ______________________________ ______________________________. Help me to respond in godly, honoring, solution-focused ways when ______________________________ says ______________________________ ______________________________. Put a guard around my lips, Holy Spirit, and the next time that happens, help me to lift it to Your hands to shape my response and turn the broken glass into a beautiful gem. In Jesus's name, amen, and Holy Spirit, I'm listening.

____

My Father's Sweater

I'm not sure how old I was when I claimed and started wearing my dad's old brown cardigan sweater. I think I was around eleven, but I do know I continued to wrap myself in it till I was fifteen. I think I must have felt like I took on something of my father's nature when I wore his sweater. It was soft with wide, flat ribs and moth holes in the sleeves, definitely not a "Mr. Rogers'" sweater, but perfect to wear on chilly nights out in the garage.

That's where you could find my dad almost every night: at his workbench repairing something one of us had broken or building something amazing. I thought my dad was the smartest man on the planet. None of my friends' fathers sent Morse code messages on a radio or made science-fiction movie sound effects with a home-built theremin. None of my friends got to watch miniature lightning shows in their garages from a Van Der Graaf generator!

Somehow I felt secure in that sweater (and in on some great secrets) standing beside my father at his workbench, even when I had to stand on tiptoe to see what he was doing. I still associate the smell of hot solder and freshly sawn wood with Dad and can hear the sound of his table saw ripping through boards on their way to becoming furniture. He built a split-level ranch-style dollhouse for me, complete with a fireplace with hand-carved "bricks," a chandelier that worked, and real tiny shingles on the roof. Dad went through several very 1960s phases, too, most of which involved the overpowering (and probably brain chemistry altering) fumes of melting plastic that became bunches of grapes and the clacking, conservation of momentum, and energy-demonstrating plastic spheres of Newton's cradle.

My father let me help him plane wood, drive nails into odd bits of scrap wood, and sweep up sawdust, all while wearing his old brown sweater. When I was a sophomore in high school, Dad helped me draw out, saw, apply a sanding sealer to, and wrap with copper wire a walnut hardwood bangle I put on a necklace that looked, very much before its time, very much like the Nike "swoosh." I felt so proud that my father was a builder and creator who guided me to create as I stood beside him, wearing his sweater, at his workbench.

Maybe those hours spent in Dad's sweater standing at his side account for some of my freedom and desire for intimacy with God, my heavenly Father. Oh, if I could, I'd love to stand beside my Father God at *His* workbench and see what *He* is creating!

Do you know what's cool? My Father God lets me help with His projects. In fact, He *wants* me to get involved! Those amazingly validating times when I get to speak some word of affirmation to another person or meet someone's need absolutely delight me because I sense that I'm standing at my Father's side and can almost see Him smile. What amazes me, though, is what God, my Father, gives me to wear while I'm at His bench: not an old brown sweater, but the righteousness of Jesus!

"God made him who had no sin to be sin for us, so that in him we might become the righteousness of God" (2 Corinthians 5:21).

"But now a righteousness from God, apart from law, has been made known, to which the Law and the Prophets testify. This righteousness from God comes through faith in Jesus Christ to all who believe" (Romans 3:21-22).

"I delight greatly in the LORD; my soul rejoices in my God. For he has clothed me with garments of salvation and arrayed me in a robe of righteousness" (Isaiah 61:10).

Today I bought three pairs of shoes for the church "Kicks for Kids" fall shoe drive for children in impoverished school districts. On learning why I was buying the shoes, the clerk at the sporting goods store gave me an extra discount. Knowing my Abba and what He likes to do in people's lives, I asked the clerk how I could pray for her and if she knew Jesus. "Well, yes...but..." she replied and then told me she'd ask prayers for her young daughter Sharon with type 1 diabetes. Aha! My Father God handed me a "board" of His word and prayer to sand, and I jumped at the chance to pray for this woman, her daughter, and whole family, and share how cherished, chosen, and beloved this woman is and how much she means to God. I believe God intended our meeting to do more than put shoes on three children; He also wanted to put His love in the heart of someone who needs to run back to her Father and needs to know He welcomes her.

> Keep reminding God's people of these things. Warn them before God against quarreling about words; it is of no value, and only ruins those who listen. Do your best to present yourself to God as one approved, a worker who does not need to be ashamed and who correctly handles the word of truth [...] In the presence of God and of Christ Jesus, who will

judge the living and the dead, and in view of his appearing and his kingdom, I give you this charge: Preach the word; be prepared in season and out of season; correct, rebuke and encourage—with great patience and careful instruction.

2 Timothy 2:14-15; 4:1-2

How many days, how many times, does God my Father hand me some work from His heart to help Him build into the life of another person? Hmm, how many times do I completely miss seeing a hammer placed in my hand, the opportunity to work beside my Father in building His kingdom in hearts and lives?

Is not this the kind of fasting I have chosen: to loose the chains of injustice and untie the cords of the yoke, to set the oppressed free and break every yoke? Is it not to share your food with the hungry and to provide the poor wanderer with shelter—when you see the naked, to clothe them, and not to turn away from your own flesh and blood? Then your light will break forth like the dawn, and your healing will quickly appear; then your righteousness will go before you, and the glory of the Lord will be your rear guard. Then you will call, and the Lord will answer; you will cry for help, and he will say: Here am I. "If you do away with the yoke of oppression, with the pointing finger and malicious talk, and if you spend yourselves in behalf of the hungry and satisfy the needs of the oppressed, then your light will rise in the darkness, and your night will become like the noonday. The Lord will guide you always; he will satisfy your needs in a sun-scorched land and will strengthen your frame. You will be like a well-watered garden, like a spring whose waters never fail. Your people will rebuild the ancient ruins and will raise up the age-old foundations; you will be called Repairer of Broken Walls, Restorer of Streets with Dwellings.

Isaiah 58:5-12

Then the angel who talked with me returned and woke me up, like someone awakened from sleep. He asked me, "What do you see?" I answered, "I see a solid gold lampstand with a bowl at the top and seven lamps on it, with seven channels to the lamps. Also there are two olive trees by it, one on the right of the bowl and the other on its left."

I asked the angel who talked with me, "What are these, my lord?"

He answered, "Do you not know what these are?"

"No, my lord," I replied.

So he said to me, "This is the word of the LORD to Zerubbabel: 'Not by might nor by power, but by my Spirit,' says the LORD Almighty.

"What are you, mighty mountain? Before Zerubbabel you will become level ground. Then he will bring out the capstone to shouts of 'God bless it! God bless it!'"

Zechariah 4:1-7

You are the salt of the earth. But if the salt loses its saltiness, how can it be made salty again? It is no longer good for anything, except to be thrown out and trampled underfoot. You are the light of the world. A town built on a hill cannot be hidden. Neither do people light a lamp and put it under a bowl. Instead they put it on its stand, and it gives light to everyone in the house. In the same way, let your light shine before others, that they may see your good deeds and glorify your Father in heaven.

Mathew 5:13-16

It takes my breath away sometimes when other people see my Father through me! Oh, God, let me stand beside You at Your workbench as You create beauty, goodness, honor, kindness, integrity, compassion, truth, love, and living faith in the lives in this world so precious to You. Guide my hands and heart and words and prayers to help You. And wow, thank You that through faith in Jesus, I get to wear a garment that looks like Your nature! You are the smartest Father in existence, and I want to be more like You. Thank You that You invite me to spend time by Your side!

A "but" to pray: Oh, Abba, Daddy, Father, You are incredible! All creation, all wisdom, all power, all authority, all goodness, all truth, all justice, all righteousness, all life comes from Your hands that are still building, repairing, restoring, and creating today and every day. I may feel small, untalented, inarticulate, incapable, *but* standing by Your side wearing *Your* righteousness, I know You're calling me to _____

_____ beside You, and I know You'll guide me as I_____

_____. Tap me on the shoulder in my spirit every time You have an opportunity for me to tell someone or show someone how much You love and care for them and give me the courage to know that, even if my words are simple, limited, or halting, or not as fancy as some others might say, and even if I don't know where in the Bible the words come from, they are still Your words sent to strengthen, build up, encourage, correct in love, restore, repair, and create a place for *Your* hands to work in another life. I give You permission to destroy my excuses right now, and here they are: _____

_____. Help me remember it's *Your* work, not mine, and *Your* Spirit, not mine, truly at work in my encounters with others; You just need me to open my mouth and open my heart so *Your* words and love can come out. I hope others see You in me! In Jesus's name, amen! Holy Spirit, I'm listening.

Lost—and Found

"Uuuuhhhh...uuuhh..." Dad's mouth opened as he tried to speak. His eyes still held that "deer in the headlights" look of incomprehension so typical of Alzheimer's patients, but I caught a spark of what, hope? Thanks? Love? Mom, my sister Bonnie, and I gathered around him, held his hands, once so strong and steady as he guided wood through the saw blade, now so forceless and weak, and touched his now thin shoulders. We'd come to say goodbye.

Two days earlier, Dad had developed pneumonia. This Monday morning, the day before Dad's seventy-fifth birthday, a nurse in the Alzheimer's unit of the nursing home called my mom to tell her to come quickly, as this might be Dad's last day. I threw the car into gear and flew to Mom's house to pick her up and quickly dash up to the home. "Oh, Rosie!" was all she could get out through her sobbing. The past five years of grieving as we watched Dad steadily decline still hadn't prepared our hearts for this day.

Surprisingly, when Mom and I arrived, Dad actually looked pretty good. He was sitting up in a chair, looking apparently healthy and much like he usually did. Mom and I chatted to him while the nurses worked around us. "To him" was all we could do because Dad hadn't been able to speak for the past two years; in fact, he hadn't even uttered so much as a syllable on the many Sundays when my husband, our ten-year-old son, and I stopped in to see him after church. Ethan had never really known Grandpa when he was well, this man who made wagons and pedal fire trucks and dollhouses and so many treasures for his grandchildren before dementia robbed him of his considerable talents.

But he was still Grandpa, still my dad, and I thought back to treasured evenings in our backyard, sitting on his telescope mount as he twirled me around the stars, or standing beside him in the garage redolent with the fragrance of newly sawn pine as he showed me how to drive a nail and drill a hole in a scrap of lumber. He was still the man I loved and respected, somewhere inside there. I dared to believe that, fought to hope it was true. As Mom and I stepped aside to let the nurse take Dad's vitals, the door opened, and my sister Bonnie walked into the room. The nurse gave a slight gasp as my dad's vital signs shot up. Bonnie hadn't seen Dad in two years, not since he moved from his home into this skilled nursing facility. She lived fifteen miles away, but it was just too painful for her to see Dad in his continually deteriorating condition. I understood completely. Bonnie had always been there for Dad and Mom over the years, and she still helped Mom every way she could.

Dad hadn't seen her in two years, yet something in him rose up in recognition of a face he loved and rose up so powerfully that his heart rate and respiration increased immediately!

"Should we pray with him? Should we tell him?" I honestly don't remember now which one of us voiced what we all were thinking: should we give Dad permission to go home to Jesus? Should we give him our blessing and love? Wordlessly we all agreed, gathered around Dad, and began to pray. "Thank you so much, Father, for our father, for his love, for the faith he shared so freely..."

Then we said it, every eye awash in tears that flowed to the nurses in the room, too. "Dad, if you're ready to go, we give you our blessing to go home to heaven."

That's when it happened: Dad tried to speak! He looked directly into our faces and said, "Uuuhhh... uuuhhhhhh." Those might have been babbled syllables to anyone else, but to the three of us, they were the voice of a beloved husband and father, struck dumb by a disease advancing brain cell by brain cell for five years, but the man was still alive and vital inside, somewhere, somehow!

One by one, we bent down and kissed him, hugged him, squeezed his feeble hand, and left, fairly confident that his healthy appearance meant this might be a false alarm. Two days later, he died, sweetly and quietly, and I believe liberated to leave the prison of his disease and to meet his fellow carpenter.

Some people might understandably dismiss this as a coincidence to which we attributed too much significance. I might, too, had it not been for a comment from one of the nurses after Dad died, and the same scene repeated exactly four weeks later over the bed of Dad's sister, my aunt Cine. Francine developed Alzheimer's two years before Dad exhibited signs of the disease. She had been bedridden, fallen away to eighty pounds, unable to walk or speak, at death's door for over a year. Mom and I went to see her on her birthday. We took her some balloons.

"Should we tell her?" Mom asked. "Should we tell her that her brother died?"

"Yes," I concurred without hesitation.

Cine was in much worse shape than Dad had been, but the day Dad died, one of the nurses on Dad's floor at his nursing home had said to me, "Your father was such a sweet, wonderful man. We enjoyed him so much." How had she known that? How can you know that about someone who can't communicate...unless Dad's spirit had been able to break out of his silence and communicate somehow, quite apart from words?

So my mother and I bent down on either side of Dad's sister, took her hands, and I softly said, "Aunt Cine, we want you to know your brother has gone on ahead of you. He's waiting for you with Jesus. If you're ready to go, we give you our permission and blessing to go home."

"Uuuhhh...uuuhhhh." Her face turned up to mine, her wild yet penetrating eyes looking directly into mine, and I knew she was there. She saw me. We kissed her and went home. So did Francine, the very next day, to her mother, her brother, her Savior, her God.

I never gave much credence to the notion that sometimes people need permission from their loved ones to leave. I always thought your body had the deciding voice in when you die. Now I'm certain that is not always the case.

Two intelligent, resourceful, achieving, loving people, struck down by a disease so heinous and hideous that it strikes terror in the hearts of most people. Any way but that one! What could possibly be the silver lining in my father's and my aunt's deaths? Simply and profoundly this: no matter what disease does to our bodies or our brains, God's spirit never leaves our spirit. We remain whole, intact, filled with all the life and love we've known and given away, whether the outside world can access it or not. And is that a meager comfort in the face of such deep loss and pain? No, even though my sister and I know we live in the shadow of DNA that may spell the same end for us, our brother suffered from undiagnosed bipolar disorder, and our mother developed vascular dementia from numerous small strokes, yet I know my spirit, and their spirits, will live eternally unchanged and unhindered. This truth is somehow a great comfort and source of hope.

> Blessed be the God and Father of our Lord Jesus Christ, the Father of mercies and God of all comfort, who comforts us in all our affliction so that we will be able to comfort those who are in any affliction with the comfort with which we ourselves are comforted by God. For just as the sufferings of Christ are ours in abundance, so also our comfort is abundant through Christ.
>
> 2 Corinthians 1:3-5 (NASB)

> If Christ is in you, though the body is dead because of sin, yet the spirit is alive because of righteousness. But if the Spirit of Him who raised Jesus from the dead dwells in you, He who raised Christ Jesus from the dead will

also give life to your mortal bodies through His Spirit who dwells in you.

Romans 8:10-11 (NASB)

On this mountain the LORD Almighty will prepare a feast of rich food for all peoples, a banquet of aged wine—the best of meats and the finest of wines. On this mountain he will destroy the shroud that enfolds all peoples, the sheet that covers all nations; he will swallow up death forever. The Sovereign LORD will wipe away the tears from all faces; he will remove his people's disgrace from all the earth. The LORD has spoken. In that day they will say, "Surely this is our God; we trusted in him, and he saved us. This is the LORD, we trusted in him; let us rejoice and be glad in his salvation."

Isaiah 25:7-9

And I will ask the Father, and he will give you another advocate (comforter) to help you and be with you forever—the Spirit of truth. The world cannot accept him, because it neither sees him nor knows him. But you know him, for he lives with you and will be in you. I will not leave you as orphans; I will come to you.

Before long, the world will not see me anymore, but you will see me. Because I live, you
also will live.

John 14:16-19

It is written: "I believed; therefore I have spoken." Since we have that same spirit of faith,
we also believe and therefore speak, because
we know that the one who raised the Lord Jesus from the dead will also raise us with Jesus
and present us with you to himself. All this
is for your benefit, so that the grace that is
reaching more and more people may cause
thanksgiving to overflow to the glory of God.
Therefore we do not lose heart. Though outwardly we are wasting away, yet inwardly we
are being renewed day by day. For our light
and momentary troubles are achieving for us
an eternal glory that far outweighs them all.
So we fix our eyes not on what is seen, but on
what is unseen, since what is seen is tempo-
rary, but what is unseen is eternal.

2 Corinthians 4:13-18

I declare to you, brothers and sisters, that
flesh and blood cannot inherit the kingdom
of God, nor does the perishable inherit the

imperishable. Listen, I tell you a mystery: We will not all sleep, but we will all be changed— in a flash, in the twinkling of an eye, at the last trumpet. For the trumpet will sound, the dead will be raised imperishable, and we will be changed. For the perishable must clothe itself with the imperishable, and the mortal with immortality. When the perishable has been clothed with the imperishable, and the mortal with immortality, then the saying that is written will come true: "Death has been swallowed up in victory. Where, O death is your victory? Where, O death, is your sting?" The sting of death is sin, and the power of sin is the law. But thanks be to God! He gives us the victory through our Lord Jesus Christ.

1 Corinthians 15:50-57

Yes, I pray researchers will home in quickly on what causes and what can cure and prevent Alzheimer's, but while I get exercise, eat a healthy diet, pray, and wait, I rest in the knowledge that who I truly am, who we truly are, both you and your loved ones who know Jesus as Lord, endures above and beyond all else. Count that as an incredible, joyful, overcoming blessing! You are never lost but ever found in the love of God!

A "but" to pray: Precious Savior Jesus, mighty God and Lord of life, Holy Spirit, thank You, thank You, that because of Jesus's death on the cross for me and because, Father, You sent Your very own Spirit to live in me when I received Your Son Jesus, my spirit is alive and will live undimmed in me forever. I know I'm getting older, and my "parts" will eventually fail, *but* my spirit _____!
These things are in my DNA: _____
_____, *but*, Holy Spirit, *You* are alive in my inmost being. Quicken *Your* life in me, and in ___
_____ as I lift him/her/them to You and ask You to fill them with Your Spirit! In Jesus's name, amen. I'm listening, Holy Spirit.

_____

Shake the Snake

Seventy-five unsupervised and rambunctiously excited kindergarteners sat in a circle on the concrete floor in the echoing auditorium, hands reaching out to touch the St. Helena mountain kingsnake I held about five inches behind its head as I walked around their group. This lithe little snake had enough and told me so—snap—in the flesh between my thumb and index finger.

Great: now I had an angry snake latched painfully firmly to my hand and wide-eyed children still waving "I want to grab you" hands. All I could think to do was try to shake off the stressed snake, hide my bleeding hand, and put the irritated reptile away. It worked until five feet later when the still-agitated snake still told me I wasn't retreating to its transport quickly enough and nailed my hand again.

This isn't the job I signed up for, I thought as I came back into the room with a cuddly by comparison hedgehog in my gloved hands. But it was exactly what I signed up for, though I never realized when I took the job at the zoo that being bitten was an occupational hazard inherent in inspiring zoo guests to amazement at the adaptations in wildlife. My praise to Jesus, I came to no harm from that serpent's two bites, and the next day the marks were as good as gone. No other snake in the program's collection ever bit or attempted to bite me.

I never dreamed of being bitten by the enemy was in the job description when I gave my life to Jesus, either. No pastor or priest ever gives the benediction, "May the Lord bless you and keep you. Beloved of God, go in peace, and now you have a target on your back," but it's true. The day I gave myself wholly and forever to God through Jesus, I crossed a line and took a side that makes the devil more than slightly agitated. The Bible describes him as a thief, serpent, or snake:

"The great dragon was hurled down—that ancient serpent called the devil, or Satan, who leads the whole world astray" (Revelation 12:9).

"The thief comes only to steal and kill and destroy; I [Jesus speaking] have come that they [we] may have life, and have it to the full" (John 10:10).

How does the snake latch on to us? The devil's venom is lies and offense: he lies about our identity, accuses us, and brings up condemnation as though the blood of Jesus isn't more than enough to truly wash away and cleanse us from all sin, injects us with offense when someone wrongs us, and plants fear that God isn't faithful to His promises, as though His Word isn't powerful and God is a liar with less than overwhelmingly loving and good plans for each of our lives.

When Peter, in his first letter to the church, exhorted believers to humble themselves before God, cast their anxiety on God, and be self-controlled and alert, he likened the devil to a prowling lion looking for someone to devour, and he was doing it then and still doing it now to believers. Peter doesn't end on that note of warning but concludes by saying, "And the God of all grace, who called you to his eternal glory in Christ, after you have suffered a little while, will himself restore you and make you strong, firm, and steadfast" (1 Peter 5:5-10).

I remembered the snake incident at the zoo in a rush of recognition that, of course, the devil isn't happy that I've forgiven my betrayer and have continued to forgive and pray for him. I must have a huge red bullseye that reads "Bite this one" on my back. Well, of course, we're targets, and the more damage we do or will inflict on the devil's plans through our forgiveness, unrelenting love, faithfulness, and praise to God, the more irritated and madder that "adder" will get. But then which do I want: to fall into bitterness to placate the devil and anger my Father and Savior, the Living God, or would I rather anger the devil and please, obey, and honor God?

The apostle Paul encountered the devil in the exact form of a poisonous snake on the island of Malta when the ship carrying him to Rome ran aground in a severe storm. Paul's companion and physician Luke recounts the incident:

> The islanders showed us unusual kindness. They built a fire and welcomed us all because it was raining and cold. Paul gathered a pile of brushwood and, as he put it on the fire, a viper, driven out by the heat, fastened itself on his hand. When the islanders saw the snake hanging from his hand, they said to each other, "This man must be a murderer; for though he escaped from the sea, Justice has not allowed him to live." But Paul shook the snake off into the fire and suffered no ill effects. The people expected him to swell up or suddenly fall dead, but after waiting a long time and seeing nothing unusual happen to him, they changed their minds and said he was a god.
>
> Acts 28:1-7

And thanks to Jesus, the devil may bite, but he can't inflict any permanent damage on us, either, when we choose to believe the truth that God's love is everlasting and His Word and character are faithful and true.

I frequently pray out of Psalm 91: "For he will command his angels concerning you to guard you in all your ways [...] You will tread on the lion and the cobra; you will trample the great lion and the serpent" (Psalm 91:11, 13). I'll "shake off the snake" of accusations and fear from the lying devourer and just tell the serpent taking aim at me to "talk to the hand!" By that, I don't mean mine, but the hand of Jesus, the hand that bears the scars of the nails that drew the blood that paid for my complete forgiveness and forever righteousness in Yeshua the Messiah, the conquering King of Kings.

> The seventy-two [disciples of Jesus, whom he had sent out to do his work] returned with joy and said, "Lord, even the demons submit to us in your name." He [Jesus] replied, "I saw Satan fall like lightning from heaven. I have given you authority to trample on snakes and scorpions and to overcome all the power of the enemy; nothing will harm you. However, do not rejoice that the spirits submit to you, but rejoice that your names are written in heaven."
>
> Luke 10:17-20

A "but" to pray: Lord God, I never wanted to become a target of Satan's anger, but being on Your side means I'm not on his. I know that means he won't be happy, *but* I know that means You *will* _____ _____ because You promise to

_____

_____. As I shake off the snake, today I tell him, "Talk to the Hand who delivers and conquers, gives me authority to command you to submit and __

_____,

and who writes my name in heaven! In Jesus's name, amen. Holy spirit, I'm listening.

_____

My Father Makes Flowers

I go deep, but I do come up for air sometimes and frankly relish the times I can feel relaxed. Even more, I enjoy the times God surprises me. I'm not a serious bike rider; my riding consisted of going up to the grocery store, riding my son down to his preschool, and then myself over to substitute teach at a local school or just riding around the neighborhood for fun. I do enjoy riding, but a nice flat bike path is my preferred route. Recently, though, I've been challenged to "kick it up a notch" and try real road biking, complete with loooooong hills.

Just getting adjusted to a much lighter bike, eleven gears I have no idea how to use, and a man's frame was challenge enough for me, much less 3–6 percent hills! I tried wearing bike shoes with cleats until the painful day early in my trial period when the sole pulled off my shoe as I tried to extract my foot from the pedal to stop. The hole in my tights slightly limited the hole in my knee...

Recently I tackled another ride with my good friend and the bicycle club he rides with. Ever the encourager, he has actually pushed me up a few hills with his hand on my back when I felt my heart rate hitting, "let's just pull over and breathe." He knows I can do it! But on Wednesday, my body decided to speak into his optimism, and after the first loooooong hill, I called over to him, "I'm taking a right here; I know how to get back to the starting point!" Before he could object—er, encourage me—strenuously, I took a right and rejoiced at the much flatter road stretching ahead.

After a quarter of a mile or so, my heart rate fell back into the "no, you're not having a heart attack" range, and even though the pavement was rough and I did feel a pang of "Quitter!" rising up in me, I was glad for the chance to breathe normally. But oh, in one mile, I knew why I chose that point to bail out of the hill conquering.

It's been a loooooong time, over five years, since anyone gave me flowers. God gave me tremendous loyalty and the spirit to pray without ceasing for His victory in a tragedy, but sometimes God's answer is, "Not in the way you hoped for." In all honesty, coming to terms with that answer has weighed on my heart on some of my rides, and carrying the weight of sorrow as well as my own body uphill on a bicycle is a load heavier than

I can bear some days. I need to be honest with you all: yes, some days my faith, like King David's in so many psalms, cries out to God, not understanding His "why." I think that was part of my bailing out on this ride.

Imagine the sweet joy, then, of the wildflowers I saw lining the road for half a mile: yellow brittlebush, burgundy Parry's penstemon, blue columbine, deep pink Baja fairy duster, orange globe mallow...I stopped pedaling, propped my bicycle against the rock wall, and stooped to smell the flowers.

My Father makes flowers! All the florists in the world can't spread out a carpet like God does. Sometimes I've marveled at the odd truth that we, humans, have a sense of beauty. We may not all agree on what makes personal beauty, or even beauty in art, but every person launched into life appreciates the splendor of stars and loveliness of flowers. And why, I wondered, did God bother to make them so lovely? So different? Some so fragrant? Yes, I know they attract bees and moths and other pollinators, but why so colorful?

Did He create them with more than pollination in mind? Why do we, women, view a gift of a bouquet, or even one single rose, as a gesture of love if God didn't put *His* love for us into their beauty?

"I am the rose of Sharon, and the lily of the valleys" (Song of Solomon 2:1, NKJV).

See how the flowers of the field grow. They do not labor or spin. Yet I tell you that not even Solomon in all his splendor was dressed like one of these. If that is how God clothes the grass of the field, which is here today and tomorrow is thrown into the fire, will he not much more clothe you—you of little faith? So do not worry, saying, "What shall we eat?" or "What shall we drink?" or "What shall we wear?" For the pagans run after all these things, and your heavenly Father knows that you need them. But seek first his kingdom and his righteousness, and all these things will be given to you as well.

Matthew 6:28-33

He was calling to me to come down that road, to rest in my Creator and Father's beauty, to receive a reminder and rest in His love through Jesus, to know most of all I am His, He is mine, and His banner over me is love:

See! The winter is past; the rains are over and gone. Flowers appear on the earth; the season of singing has come, the cooing of doves is heard in our land. The fig tree forms its early fruit, the blossoming vines spread their fra-

grance. Arise, come, my darling; my beautiful
one, come with me.

Song of Songs 2:11-13

He extends the single stem of the blood-red rose of
Sharon in love to you today.

A "but" to pray: Rose of Sharon, Lily of the Valley,
even if someone *has* given me flowers recently, and
even if *no one* has given me flowers, You are the flower
and fragrance sweetly blooming in my life. Is my life a
sweet fragrance lifted up to You, too? I may never have
realized it, *but* let me hear Your thoughts toward me __

_____

_____. And, my Beloved, how
can I be a pleasing fragrance to You today? Whom can
I love, where can I serve, whom can I help, where can I
put myself: at work or at the grocery store or at school
or in my neighborhood today? _____

_____

_____. I pray You to make my life the aroma of Christ
wherever I go, and with Your help, I won't wait for a
special occasion to be the flower in someone's day. In
Jesus's name, amen. Holy Spirit, I'm listening.

_____

The Painted Pickle Jar

One of my greatest treasures is the "jewelry box" my younger son made for me from popsicle sticks: the lid has a wooden bead for a "handle," and the interior is lined with a square of red felt, roughly the same dimensions as the bottom of the box. Why on earth are fifty popsicle sticks so precious to me? Because the shape they took and the gift they are came from a heart and life precious to me. Ethan gave me the best he could create from fifty popsicle sticks, glue, a bead, and felt. His heart is the treasure; the box is a reflection of his love.

Mommies get it. Maybe daddies do too. I know this for a fact, but more importantly, what I realized this morning is that same joy in God's heart when we craft our lives for Him. Before this sounds too lofty and climbs too high, let me ground it in what I see so clearly now that I didn't see when I was five years old.

Sunday school, Mason, Ohio, just before Easter in 1955, me five years old. All I brought was a pickle jar. Our craft was painting a jar with tempera paint to make a "vase" to hold one jonquil bulb, an Easter gift for our mothers. Limited eye-hand coordination in us all, we stroked our glass jars with chubby paintbrushes and watery tempera in spring colors. I can still feel the cool of the glass, the rough edges of flaking paint on my paintbrush, see the dribbles running down the jar and onto the newspaper on the table, smell the chalky, rich odor of the paint. Mine was going to be yellow, like a golden jonquil flower. Of course, the paint didn't stick very well, and in many places, the clear glass showed through, but I reveled in the transformation happening under my hand.

I suspect we had a Bible story lesson while our jars dried, or we might have had to wait till the next Sunday to pour tiny stones, pebbles would be too glorified a term for what we used, more like the ballast along the railroad track that ran about 500 feet behind our house, into the jars to support the single bulb we placed inside. Water came next, then anchoring the jonquil bulb flat end down in the stones.

I was so happy to carry the gift downstairs and thrust it up into my mother's hands! I'd made something to give my mommy joy! Mom must have read the "Mommy Manual" or internalized it from her jolly, loving, short but ample-lapped mother who was my Grandma Miner, so of course, when we got home, she placed it in the sunny window above the sink in the kitchen, a place of honor if ever there was one, where she could watch the shoot, the leaves, the stem, then the flower gloriously unfold in the weak Ohio spring sunshine.

What on earth does this have to do with God? Sixty years later, it hit me on a windy, drizzly Arizona morning that I didn't give my mother anything from my own resources; someone else supplied everything I gave her, even though I regarded the gift as mine and found great pleasure, delight, and value in being able to create and give a gift to my mother.

This morning I look back on everything I've been blessed to "give to God": the messages I've spoken, the Sunday school and vacation Bible school classes I taught, the youth ministry and prayer teams I led, the books I helped my senior pastor write, the stories I wrote that ended up in Chicken Soup for the Soul books, the leader and study guides I've written, the sons I poured my time and energies and love into, the marriage I tried to do the same in, the people I've prayed with and for (Gosh, don't I sound wonderful?), and I realize with a shock or revelation piercing deep into the core of me down to my five-year-old true self that *I didn't bring any of my own resources to anything I've ever "given" God!*

In 1864, William W. How penned the words to a hymn we used to sing in church every Sunday after the offering was taken up front to the altar:

> We give Thee but Thine own,
> Whate'er the gift may be;
> All that we have is Thine alone,
> A trust, O Lord, from Thee.

Did any of us mean what we were perfunctorily singing? Wasn't it more a case of, "I worked hard for this money, so God, I'm going to give You a bit of it; good, giving person that I am, I feel proud of myself for being so generous. I hope You're pleased with me for giving You what I earned! "

Hmmm...God created my body and my brain, the wiring in me that sees analogies and relationships, the eye-hand coordination I have and the joy I get in making things with my hands, the mental aha to see ways I can use junk, the limited courage I have to stand up in front of people and open my mouth, the very thoughts I have and nudges I get *all come from God, to begin with!* I don't give Him anything that isn't His first, in fact, His gifts to me!

When King David dedicated offerings brought to build the Temple in Jerusalem, he offered up the truth:

Whoever possessed precious stones gave them to the treasury of the house of the LORD, in care of Jehiel the Gershonite. Then the people rejoiced because they had offered so willingly, for they made their offering to the LORD with a whole heart, and King David also rejoiced greatly. So David blessed the LORD in the sight of all the assembly; and David said, "Blessed are You, O LORD God of Israel our father, forever and ever. Yours, O LORD, is the greatness and the power and the glory and the victory and the majesty, indeed everything that is in the heavens and the earth; yours is the dominion, O LORD, and you exalt yourself as head over all. Both riches and honor come from you, and you rule over all, and in your hand is power and might; and it lies in your hand to make great and to strengthen everyone. Now, our God, we give you thanks, and praise your glorious name. But who am I, and who are my people, that we should be able to give as generously as this? Everything comes from you, and we have given you only what comes from your hand. We are foreigners and strangers in your sight, as were all our ancestors. Our days on earth are like a shadow, without hope. Lord our God,

all this abundance that we have provided for
building you a temple for your Holy Name
comes from your hand, and all of it belongs
to you."

1 Chronicles 29:8-16 (NASB)

Oh, the five-year-old in each one of us, but oh, the
lavishly loving God who remarkable receives what we
give Him and treasures it as much as I treasure my popsicle stick jewelry box, as much as my mom treasured
her painted pickle jar, because, against all common
sense, He treasures us! I only hope that, like the loving
Dad I know He is, God has received all the clay figurines
and popsicle stick creations and painted pickle jars I've
given Him with, and honestly, this is true, the same delight I felt in giving my mother the pickle jar. Maybe
now I can appreciate my mother's receiving that jar as
a great gift to me. Maybe now I can see being that privileged to get to use His gifts to make something I hope
and pray makes a difference to and in other lives in this
world is, in fact, a gift God gave to me.

"To the LORD your God belong the heavens, even the
highest heavens, the earth and everything in it" (Deuteronomy 10:14).

"The earth is the LORD'S, and all it contains, the
world, and those who dwell in it" (Psalm 24: 1 NASB).

Ah, Abba, do You have tempera paint in heaven? Can I make You a vase for a flower to grow in Your throne room? Thank You that You give me so much. May I turn as much as I can into treasures for You, but may I always remember they come from Your heart of love and grace into my chubby fingers.

A "but" to pray: God, Daddy, Father, everything I have and am and ever hope to be is all a gift from You. I can't take credit for anything other than what I do with what You give me, and even those opportunities are gifts from You. I may not be anything in the world's eyes, or I may daily hear the praise of other people, *but* it's Your praise, after all. I may have much or I may have little, *but* God, thank You that You receive my

_____ and say _____

_____. I hope it grows in Your kitchen window to be something of beauty and fragrance for You. In Jesus's name, amen. Holy Spirit, I'm listening.

Sticks and Stones

(Note: I am not suggesting anyone endure physical, mental, or emotional abuse. Be safe and get help, please!)

"Sticks and stones will break my bones, but words will never hurt me," was what we resorted to in the face of taunts and teasing from the other children on the playground. They would, of course, never have the courage to be verbally abusive, and that's what it was, in front of the teacher or principal, because they'd face the consequences of disrespecting another person. In my day, that was one quick, solid whack from Mr. Nelson's paddle. Interestingly, one swat often "redirected" the bullies in a class far more effectively than a time out in the corner.

The truth is, words cut and injure more deeply, significantly, and for much longer than any poke from a stick or bruise from a stone. Sticks and stones hurt the body, which mends quickly. Words cut viciously into the heart, into the soul, into the identity and value of a person, which means so much to God. No one, not even my enemy, deserves to be dismissed as a person robbed of value, dignity, honor, respect.

I grew up in a home where harsh words were never used or heard. I only knew of abuse, or domestic violence, as hurtful physical acts, and that never happened in our home or, as far as I knew, in the homes of my friends. Oh, yes, my mother let me know when I'd disobeyed, but she always spoke about my behavior, not of me as a person. I never doubted my worth to her, a value she made all the more evident the day she came to ask me to forgive her for falsely accusing me of lying. What worth she poured into me that day!

So I was never prepared to recognize or deal with verbal abuse when it struck suddenly like the fangs of a small, hidden viper early in my marriage. Had I known then what I came to know thirty-eight years later, I would have confronted the angry jabs at my identity as the abuse they were. I chalked it up to my husband's early childhood, living in a very strict family, and let it roll off my back. Only much later did his mother tell her children that their father was seriously mentally ill. Only later did she reveal her frustration and her own sense of invalidation to me. I had no idea then the biological mechanics of how early emotional and verbal abuse permanently damages "wiring" in the brain and sets up a child to become a "user," "controller," or abuser later in life.

God does not want anyone abused verbally, mentally, emotionally, or physically. Anger is an emotion God gave us to alert us to problems. Righteous anger is not sinful and should not be associated with abuse. Anger, if mishandled, can certainly lead to a sinful, abusive response, but it is a sinful heart, not the emotion of anger, that is the root cause of abuse. Abuse crosses the line from the proper expression of unmet needs to a sinful disregard for the worth and dignity of another person. The Bible regards abuse as sin because we are called to love one another (John 13:34). Abuse disregards others and violates this command. An abuser desires to satisfy his natural selfishness regardless of the consequences to himself or others.

The Bible doesn't use the term "verbal abuse," but God speaks clearly about the power of our words: "The tongue has the power of life and death" (Proverbs 18:21).

Verbal abuse is one weapon in the stockpile of emotional abuse. While abusers use many tactics and strategies, the ultimate goal is to gain dominance and control over someone in a relationship. We all can be or have been abusive at some time because we all fall short of God's command to love one another at all times, and I'll be the first to admit that some much less than loving words have come out of my mouth to the very people I love most, but chronic, ongoing verbal, emotional, or mental abuse is a sign of a much deeper issue or pervasive sin problem. Verbal abuse constitutes psychological violence. Verbal abuse is a habitual sin that seldom goes away on its own and can potentially escalate into physical or other forms of abuse.

Those who've been abused don't get a free pass to perpetuate it in their own relationships. Those of us who tend toward deep empathy need to walk away from the false sense of responsibility for, or the need to cover up, an abuser's actions; sometimes being "nice" isn't helpful or healing, nor is it, I've come to see, truly "Christian." It only puts a Band-Aid over a festering wound that needs to be exposed to the light of truth for real cleansing. The tricky part is to understand how to "speak the truth in love" and how to walk away in integrity without returning abuse for abuse when the truth is rejected.

Christians, churches, and civil authorities clearly know what to tell victims of physical abuse: get out while you can and report it. Sticks and stones leave marks. But how can the abused document verbal, emotional, or mental abuse? Who will believe you when your abuser seems so charming and mentally sound? Where do you go for help? And why do I include this in a devotional book? Because God cares about and loves both the abused and their abusers, and we have an agape love responsibility to both.

God does indeed know the truth, and I cling to the truth that God will never abandon me—even if on my rough days I feel like He has—or grow tired of loving me, or ever tell me I'm not enough. I stand completely in awe, in fact, of His hand leading me. Out of relentless love and value for me, God connected me in convoluted ways I could have never orchestrated with people who brought me His word, wisdom, and His encouragement. Through, of all things, pouring a cup of hot cider for a stranger at a Christmas party, God connected me with a man who led a small group Bible study at another church. In that group, I met a woman (she, ironically, got the job I had interviewed for) well versed in emotional disorders, who told me quite calmly but bluntly one evening exactly what I didn't have the knowledge to identify, and then pointed me to a helpful website, BPDCentral.com. God opened my eyes to understand things that had confused me in my marriage for decades. God's intervention brought me release from false blame but also understanding that gave me deep compassion and protected me from bitterness.

God spoke through another woman who didn't even know me but who heard words for me from the Holy Spirit as she was ironing and gave the message to the young man who was renting a room in my house. I share it to encourage someone else who is suffering the pain of abuse and injustice: "Don't give up. Come to Me in My secret hiding place, under My protective wings. Love Me as I love you. Fear not anything man has done to you. My Word is what is important. I hold you in My arms. You are My chosen child."

On the Saturday between Good Friday and Easter Sunday last year, God lovingly lined up three cars with "vanity plates," license plates with words or a reference to a saying, to pull in front of my car one after the other. In order, the plates read "Justice," "Christ," and "Chronos." Never before or since have even two cars with plates that made a phrase lined up in front of me! Oh, God, You do see and know, and You have a time of redemptive judgment ahead. Those who take You, Jesus, as Savior, also take Your blood as our defense, Your righteousness imputed to us as our defender.

But believers, can we as the church, we as Christians, wake up to the silent suffering going on in our midst, drop the shame and blame we often lay on the victims—as if they were responsible for creating the abuse in their abusers—and offer them true grace, safety, and a place of healing? Can we courageously confront in redemptive love the people inflicting abuse out of their own unconfessed and hidden wounding? Can we offer the wounded abusers a place of real grace and tough but genuine love that gives hope for healing and transformation when they find the courage to admit their abusive nature and ask for help? We must break the silence to end the wounding!

I pray we can. I pray others caught in the trap of unseen abuse will find the courage to speak to someone of their own gender whom they can trust and seek wise counsel. I pray Christians will offer better, more compassionate and understanding advice than others gave me: "Just get over it." I pray we can all know who our true enemy is: Satan and his legion of abusive deceivers. I pray for my abuser that somehow the relentless love of God will pursue him with redemptive judgment, not for his destruction, but for his transformation. My prayer for a narcissist, "God, break him to make him the man of true goodness, kindness, and integrity you intended him to be when you formed him, in his mother's womb," is not a prayer of anger or revenge, but a fervent cry for true justice for us all from the real abuser of us all, Satan himself, the father of lies and abuse. Father, I surrender my abuser to You for Your victory over the abuser in him.

> You have heard that it was said, "Love your neighbor and hate your enemy." But I tell you, love your enemies and pray for those who persecute you, that you may be children of your Father in heaven.
>
> Matthew 5:43

"Reckless words pierce like a sword, *but* the tongue of the wise brings healing" (Proverbs 12:18, emphasis mine).

> Brood of vipers! How can you, being evil, speak good things? For out of the abundance of the heart the mouth speaks. A good man out of the good treasure of his heart brings forth good things, and an evil man out of the evil treasure brings forth evil things. But I say to you that for every idle word men may speak, they will give account of it in the day of judgment. For by your words you will be justified, and by your words you will be condemned.
>
> Matthew 12:34-37 (NKJV)

> Bless those who persecute you; bless and do not curse. Rejoice with those who rejoice; mourn with those who mourn. Live in harmony with one another. Do not be proud, but be willing to associate with people of low position. Do not be conceited. Do not repay anyone evil for evil. Be careful to do what is right in the eyes of everyone. If it is possible, as far as it depends on you, live at peace with everyone. Do not take revenge, my dear friends, but leave room for God's wrath, for it is writ-

ten: "It is mine to avenge; I will repay," says the Lord.

Romans 12:14-19

A "but" to pray: Oh, God, Abba, Father, I cry out to You. You feel my pain from _____

_____

_____, and You want me, above all, to know how much You love me. I confess I've been thoughtless and I hurt _____'s feelings when I _____

_____. Forgive me, God, and give me the courage to go to _____ admit my wrong, and ask for forgiveness. God, You know that _____ did/said _____

_____, and I see now that wasn't just a mistake; it was abuse. Holy Spirit, show me if and how and where and to whom I need to speak up to bring into the open, for true healing, and if I have been abusive in my words, O God of mercy, forgive me, give me the grace to go to those I've wounded to confess it as sin and ask their forgiveness, and guide me to good sound counsel so I can be cleansed and healed. _____

_____. Show me what real love looks like in this situation, and where and how I need to exercise "tough love" if that's what will be best. Almighty God, if I need to walk away from _____

_____, give me the courage to trust that You will hold me in Your hand, cover me with Your promises, and provide for my needs as Your Word promises. I'm listening for Your voice now, looking for Your hand to lead me. Help me trust in Your love for me. In Jesus's name, amen! Holy Spirit, I'm listening.

Standing on His Feet—er, Promises

No clear path, everything that seemed promising turned into a short walk to a false hope, every interview turned into a discouraging "You were our second choice," too much unsettled, and my life hinging on what I can't make happen for myself. I want to follow God's will, and the last thing I want to do is start whacking in panic through the underbrush of the tangle that is my life right now with an "I guess I'll have to do it myself" mental machete. It seems I've done that and only wandered my way further off the trail, deeper into disappointments that feel every bit like a detour from God's intention for my life. At least I hope He intended good for me, but when the lyrics of an old song, "God will make a way where there seems to be no way," sound more like a taunt than encouragement, what is a person of faith to do?

In incredible opposition to our western culture of self-reliance and self-determination, I think some of the sweetest words to God's ears must surely be "Father, I *can't!*" As I threw my hands heavenward in complete frustration and defeat today, what floated down was one of my earliest delights as a small child: reaching up to put my hands in my dad's, planting my feet on his big shoes, and going for a ride on my father's feet. It's vaguer than a memory, nothing but a wisp of simple knowing, but I know I felt treasured and safe then, before the harsh realities of the world threw me off balance. My daddy wouldn't walk me off a cliff or into oncoming traffic; he knew where he was going, and he was having fun taking me for a ride. I sensed his pleasure in this act of trusting bonding. A decal on the rear window of a car in front of me this morning reinforced the message: "Semper Fi—always faithful."

I witnessed the same kind of trusting bonding with our first dog Amy, decades ago. A tiny mutt puppy, the black speck of fur that she was all but disappeared into knee-deep Michigan snow with every bound as she plowed ahead of us, trying to break trail. Her strength gave out in just a few hundred yards, and what she did next both completely surprised me and convinced me she possessed uncanny intelligence: Amy turned and leaped directly onto my husband's snowshoes, landing and looking up with trusting puppy eyes as if knowing where greater strength, direction, and security lay.

"I tried it my way in my strength. That didn't work at all the way I planned. Now take me where you want to go." I still have those snowshoes in the garage here in the desert, a reminder to me that I have a place to rest when my "woof" is worn out.

How often I wish I had the simple trust of a dog or a three-year-old! Because I wish I did, I decided to do something radical today after yet another job interview: I reached my arms up again and curved my fingers around two unseen and unfelt hands that once were stained with rivers of blood, picked up my right foot, then my left, and in my choosing planted my feet on the two that walked on water.

For me, I sense that my struggle of past years is largely about *Him*, about *God*, and who I believe He is. Maybe I'm a test case, and this life of mine merely records some experimental data. This is Your journey, too, Jesus. I'm pretty sure the only way I can keep my feelings from straying off the trail, away from what God wants for me, is to "stand on His feet" and let Him do some walking for me. It would be totally crazy if I didn't recognize—or in this season, against all the earthly evidence to the contrary just decide to believe—that God is my loving Father, that He knows where He's going, and it isn't off a cliff. If I can't trust the economy, if I can't trust my resume or online job search engines (which all too frequently post jobs that have already been filled), I guess I'm going to have to, and will be wiser to, trust my heavenly Father.

How odd will it be if this is what He's been waiting for: to delight in taking me for a ride on His feet and bonding us so closely that I'll take this memory of His pleasure into eternity when I really see His smile.

> They will come with weeping, they will pray as I bring them back. I will lead them beside streams of water on a level path where they will not stumble, because I am Israel's [and my] father.
>
> Jeremiah 31:9

"He will not let your foot slip" (Psalm 121:3).

"If the LORD delights in a [wo]man's way, he makes his steps firm; though he stumble, he will not fall, for the LORD upholds him with his hand" (Psalm 37:23).

A "but" to pray: God, this may be the craziest thing I've ever done. It certainly seems senseless, but I have to admit that I can't make any change or dent or progress in _____, *but* here goes: I'm going to reach up for Your hands, plant my feet on Your big shoes, and trust You to take me _____ _____. I'd love to hear Your chuckle as You lead me to _____

_____

_____. Thank You that Your feet are big enough to take my weight, Your hands strong enough to hold me up, Your eyes keen enough to see the way to walk me right into Your will and purposes for me. In Jesus's name, amen. Holy Spirit, I'm listening.

_____

I Would Be True

In my quiet time this morning—and boy, does God go to work on me—I see so clearly that you, who are reading this, want and need what we all want and need; you want to feel wanted and need to be needed. Pop psychology, Oprah, and Dr. Phil, to the contrary: it isn't healthy to be so independent and walled in by boundaries that we "don't need anyone else for our happiness." That's simply not true. True, we need healthy boundaries to keep out harmful influences, but total independence builds walls around us that keep out the need for the love God created in us, both as givers and receivers.

I am a "traditional" woman with traditional values, born into a less competitive and compulsive culture and into a time when relationships mattered more than accomplishment. I recognize the influence of my culture and family, and I don't apologize for being myself. Yes, we are all influenced by the culture and the era in which we grew up and in which we live, but we don't have to be shaped by those times, expectations, and distortions.

My worth doesn't come from being "hip" to culture or making money or being in an influential job or looking like the models and stars on television or in magazines; my worth comes from being true to myself, the person God created me to be: alive, loving, passionate, compassionate, open, giving, and forgiving. Those are God's values, not culture's, and those values are timeless. I choose to keep my heart free from the schemes of perversion and distortion of what's important and lasting, even when those come in contemporary cultural wrappings.

> But who are you, a human being, to talk back to God? Shall what is formed say to the one who formed it, "Why did you make me like this?" Does not the potter have the right to make out of the same lump of clay some pottery for special purposes and some for common use? What if God, although choosing to show his wrath and make his power known, bore with great patience the objects of his wrath—prepared for destruction? What if he did this to make the riches of his glory known to the objects of his mercy, whom he prepared in advance for glory—even us, whom he also called, not only from the Jews but also from the Gentiles? As he says in Hosea: "I will

call them 'my people' who are not my people;
and I will call her 'my loved one' who is not my
loved one," and, in the very place where it was
said to them, "You are not my people," there
they will be called "children of the living God."

Romans 9:20-26

Contrary to what people might think, what my children remember isn't going to exotic places for vaca-
tions or all the gadgets and technology we bought them.
They remember camping out in the backyard to watch
lunar eclipses, playing board games, reading bedtime
stories, running through the backyard sprinklers, the
sheets I hung up outside for them to paint on with wa-
tercolors, then wash off with the hose, the letters I se-
cretly wrote them from their "imaginary friends" and
put under their bedroom doors in the mornings, leaf
boats we sailed down rainwater in the gutters, olive and
green pepper faces I made on their sandwiches (and on
my husband's because he needed love in his lunch, too),
and fun notes I put in their lunch boxes.

I hope what my friends remember are the times we
laughed together, looked each other in the eyes, hugged
and cried together, picnics and baking parties we had,
Christmas decorations and crafts we made together in
each other's homes, the silly day we sat in the backyard
with cucumber slices on our eyes and yogurt and hon-

ey on our faces, the times we made "Joy boxes" to take to people in hospitals or going through hard times, all of us just being ourselves true to our hearts and each other.

I enjoy contemporary worship songs and even the "smoke and lights and mirrors" that seem omnipresent in worship services now, and old hymns from a hundred years before I was born still bring me to my feet and bring me to tears. I am gratified that when I teach children, I'm able to bring creativity into the mix to help them learn and have fun. I am amazed that I've been able to present workshops and write books that touched people's lives in uplifting, encouraging ways. That kind of work mattered to me. The constant in everything that touched and touches me is God's relentless love and unchanging grace, glad presence, great power, and mercy.

I have a self to be true to: not so I shine, but so Jesus shines through me. You have a self to be true to as well and your own unique way to reflect God's love and goodness, strength and hope in your corner of the world. No one else can be who you are, do what you do, say what you can say out of your heart, reach where you reach, reflect the colors of God out of your experience, or love as you love.

You heavens above, rain down my righteousness; let the clouds shower it down. Let the earth open wide, let salvation spring up, let righteousness flourish with it; I, the Lord, have created it. Woe to those who quarrel with their Maker, those who are nothing but potsherds among the potsherds on the ground. Does the clay say to the potter, "What are you making?" Does your work say, "The potter has no hands?" Woe to the one who says to a father, "What have you begotten?" or to a mother, "What have you brought to birth?" This is what the Lord says—the Holy One of Israel, and its Maker: Concerning things to come, do you question me about my children, or give me orders about the work of my hands? It is I who made the earth and created mankind on it. My own hands stretched out the heavens; I marshaled their starry hosts.

Isaiah 45:8-12

The unalterable truth of who you are and who I am in Jesus Christ is:

I am God's child (John 1:12).

I have been justified (Romans 5:1).

I am Christ's friend (John 15:15).

I belong to God (1 Corinthians 6:20).

I am a member of Christ's body (1 Corinthians 12:27).

I am assured all things work together for good (Romans 8:28).

I have been established, anointed, and sealed by God (2 Corinthians 1:21-22).

I am a citizen of heaven (Philippians 3:20).

I am hidden with Christ in God (Colossians 3:3).

I have not been given a spirit of fear but of power, love, and self-discipline (2 Timothy 1:7).

I am born of God, and the evil one cannot touch me (1 John 5:18).

I am blessed in the heavenly realms with every spiritual blessing (Ephesians 1:3).

I am chosen before the creation of the world (Ephesians 1:4, 11).

I am holy and blameless (Ephesians 1:4).

I am adopted as His child (Ephesians 1:5).

I am given God's glorious grace lavishly and without restriction (Ephesians 1:5, 8).

I am in Him (Ephesians 1:7; 1 Corinthians 1:30).

I have redemption (Ephesians 1:8).

I am forgiven (Ephesians 1:8; Colossians 1:14).

I have a purpose (Ephesians 1:9 & 3:11).

I have hope (Ephesians 1:12).

I am included (Ephesians 1:13).

Today I have to ask myself what's more important and what gives value to my life: what I have in my house and in my bank account and on my resume and on the nameplate on my desk, if I sit at one, or what and who I have in my heart? What comes into my hands or what comes out of my life? I would be true, even as the old hymn proclaims:

I would be true, for there are those who trust me;
I would be pure, for there are those who care;
I would be strong, for there is much to suffer;
I would be brave, for there is much to dare;
I would be brave, for there is much to dare.
I would be friend of all—the foe, the friendless;
I would be giving, and forget the gift;
I would be humble, for I know my weakness;
I would look up, and laugh, and love and lift.
I would look up, and laugh, and love and lift.

Words by Howard A. Walter, 1906

Therefore, I urge you, brothers and sisters, in view of God's mercy, to offer your bodies as a living sacrifice, holy and pleasing to God— this is your true and proper worship. Do not conform to the pattern of this world, but be transformed by the renewing of your mind. Then you will be able to test and approve what

God's will is—his good, pleasing and perfect will.

For by the grace given me I say to every one of you: Do not think of yourself more highly than you ought, but rather think of yourself with sober judgment, in accordance with the faith God has distributed to each of you. For just as each of us has one body with many members, and these members do not all have the same function, so in Christ we, though many, form one body, and each member belongs to all the others. We have different gifts, according to the grace given to each of us. If your gift is prophesying, then prophesy in accordance with your faith; if it is serving, then serve; if it is teaching, then teach; if it is to encourage, then give encouragement; if it is giving, then give generously; if it is to lead, do it diligently; if it is to show mercy, do it cheerfully.

Love must be sincere. Hate what is evil; cling to what is good. Be devoted to one another in love. Honor one another above yourselves. Never be lacking in zeal, but keep your spiritual fervor, serving the Lord. Be joyful in hope, patient in affliction, faithful in prayer. Share with the Lord's people who are in need. Practice hospitality. Bless those who persecute you; bless and do not curse. Rejoice with those who rejoice; mourn with those who mourn. Live in harmony with one another. Do not be proud, but be willing to associate with people of low position. Do not be conceited. Do not repay anyone evil for evil. Be careful to do what is right in the eyes of everyone. If it is possible, as far as it depends on you, live at peace with everyone.

Romans 12:1-18

God said it of you and me: your life matters to God, just as you are. Whether you do anything *for* Him or not, God loves you, *but* yes, He'd love to help you fulfill the purposes He created you for, raise you up to all He placed and saw and sees in you, and find and feel great satisfaction in being the truest to God's design you that you can be, regardless of the era or culture you live in. You are the called out, the chosen, *His*.

I thank my God every time I remember you. In all my prayers for all of you, I always pray with joy because of your partnership in the gospel from the first day until now, being confident of this, that he who began a good work in you will carry it on to completion until the day of Christ Jesus.

Philippians 1:3-6

A "but" to pray: Oh, Father, I know I let other people influence me too much, more than I let Your Word and Your values influence me, and I let my culture's values tell me who I am, more than I listen for Your voice. I do have to live where I am, in the time I am, but God, help me see who *You* created me to be, and help me shift from _____ to _____
_____. Help me value _____

_____

_____ and be patient in_____

_____

____. Where do I need You to change me into the "me" You see and want me to be? _____
_____. Help me, Father, to bless _____ by_____

_____

__. Most of all, help me *know* how much You have invested Your love and grace into me, shape me for Your purposes, so I can hold my head up and know that I am

_____

____. In Jesus's name, amen and hooray! Holy Spirit, I'm listening.

_____

No Pigs Allowed!

A sacred space. So very different from the way 99 percent of our culture views the physical relationship between a husband and wife, a man and a woman in covenant, but I awoke literally to that understanding. When I spoke my covenant promise forty-five years ago, I meant it and intended to keep it, "For richer, for poorer, in sickness and health, for better or for worse, forsaking all others keep myself only unto him so long as we both shall live." Many churches in the Christian community consider marriage a sacrament, right alongside communion and, for some, baptism.

Here is a full definition of "sacrament" according to Merriam-Webster:

> 1a: a Christian rite (as baptism or the Eucharist) that is believed to have been ordained by Christ and that is held to be a means of divine grace or to be a sign or symbol of a spiritual reality. [7]

Directly from Latin, *sacramentum* is "a consecrating"; "sacred" directly from Latin *sacrare*—"to make sacred," "consecrate," "hold sacred," "immortalize," "set apart," "dedicate."

This I know is true from Scripture: when I received Jesus as my personal Lord and Savior, God's spirit lives in me.

> But if Christ is in you, then even though your body is subject to death because of sin, the Spirit gives life because of righteousness. And if the Spirit of him who raised Jesus from the dead is living in you, he who raised Christ from the dead will also give life to your mortal bodies because of his Spirit who lives in you.
>
> Romans 8:10-11

> Do you not know that your bodies are members of Christ? Shall I then take the members of Christ and make them members of a prostitute? Never! Or do you not know that he who is joined to a prostitute becomes one body with her? For, as it is written, "The two will become one flesh." But he who is joined to the Lord becomes one spirit with him. Flee from sexual immorality. Every other sin a person commits is outside the body, but the

sexually immoral person sins against his own body. Or do you not know that your body is a temple of the Holy Spirit within you, whom you have from God? You are not your own, for you were bought with a price. So glorify God in your body.

1 Corinthians 6:15-20 (ESV)

I'd been Christian a long time before I recognized the truth that, when we are joined with Jesus, our body becomes the dwelling place of God's Holy Spirit. In truth, our heart becomes a type of the Holy of Holies, the place in the physical Temple where God's spirit dwelt, the place where only a consecrated priest could enter at specified times to meet with God.

This lives, alive in spirit and, I think, in real, tangible truth, in marriage between two Christians. Even for two human beings who aren't Christian, physical union creates a spiritual reality:

The man said, "This is now bone of my bones, and flesh of my flesh; She shall be called Woman, because she was taken out of Man." For this reason a man shall leave his father and his mother, and be joined to his wife; and they shall become one flesh.

Genesis 2:24 (NASB)

Married, when we came together in the physical bond of intimacy, we created a spiritual bond as well, and oneness in spirit even truer than the physical union. If our bodies were the Temple of the Holy Spirit who lives in us, then that union creates a sacred space where the Holy Spirit in him joined the Holy Spirit in me—a consecration, held dedicated, set apart, a means of divine grace—expressing a spiritual reality in physicality. That was God's intent for marriage from the beginning of creation.

God's Temple was meant to be and remain undefiled, a holy space set apart for man to meet with God. Nothing unclean was allowed in the Temple, particularly in the Holy of Holies. But enter the Greek Antiochus IV, the eighth ruler of the Seleucid Empire centered in Babylonia and covering the eastern part of Alexander the Great's former empire. He gave himself the surname "Epiphanes," which means "the visible god" (that he and Jupiter were identical). He acted as though he really were Jupiter, and the people called him "Epimanes," meaning "the madman." He was violently bitter against the Jews and was determined to exterminate them and their religion. He devastated Jerusalem in 168 BC, defiled the Temple, offered a pig on its altar, erected an altar to Jupiter, prohibited Temple worship, forbade circumcision on pain of death, sold thousands of Jewish families into slavery, destroyed all copies of Scripture that could be found, and slaughtered everyone discovered in possession of such copies, and resorted to every conceivable torture to force Jews to renounce their religion. This led to the Maccabaean revolt, one of the most heroic feats in history.

What in the world does Hellenistic history have to do with marital intimacy? Simply put: no pigs on the altar. We bring pigs into the sacred space of our covenantal union when we bring in corruption and loose standards from popular culture, when thoughts of being with anyone other than our marriage partner enter our minds, when we set any "unclean thing" before our eyes other than our spouse and the sacredness of that person's body and spirit.

I always wanted to write, and decades ago, I began composing a romance novel in my mind. I set out the plot, the setting, and the characters...until I saw the trap I could easily have fallen into. I could have created a male character, a hero so perfect in my eyes that the value, worth, and person of my own husband might have begun to diminish in my thoughts and eventually in my heart. A pig on the altar. Immediately I dropped the idea. No one and nothing was going to take the place of my husband in my thoughts, affections, or body, period, not even if what I was creating was a work of fantasy. He was God's gift to me; God's spirit lived in him, and bringing anything else into our relationship was, to me, tantamount to bringing a pig into the Holy of Holies.

"Let marriage be held in honor among all, and let the marriage bed be undefiled, for God will judge the sexually immoral and adulterous" (Hebrews 13:4, ESV).

> So you also must consider yourselves dead to sin and alive to God in Christ Jesus. Let not sin therefore reign in your mortal body, to make you obey its passions. Do not present your members to sin as instruments for unrighteousness, but present yourselves to God as those who have been brought from death to life, and your members to God as instruments for righteousness. For sin will have no dominion over you, since you are not under law but under grace.
>
> Romans 6:11-14 (ESV)

Though I didn't mind my children watching cartoons on the small TV set in our bedroom if the big one in the family room was tuned in to other programing, my other half regarded our bedroom as a space off-limits to our children. Agreeably more off-limits than that room, however, were both of our bodies, reserved for each other alone, held apart, sacred, and meant to be consecrated to each other alone.

Yes, sexual intimacy is meant to be pleasurable, enjoyable, even fun, but above all and surrounding all, sexual intimacy creates a sacred space between two people. I've found few in the world of online dating who believe this is true, but I know in the core of my being that it is meant to be so—a sacred space—by the One who created our sexuality, to begin with. All you have to do is read the Song of Songs in the Bible to know that God didn't create sexual intimacy to be something stuffy and ethereal; He meant it to be physical and spiritual at the same time.

"Keep steady my steps according to your promise, and let no iniquity get dominion over me" (Psalm 119:133, ESV).

"I will refuse to look at anything vile and vulgar. I hate all who deal crookedly; I will have nothing to do with them" (Psalm 101:3, NLT).

Pornography: a pig in the Holy of Holies. Thoughts straying to anyone else: a pig in the Holy of Holies. Selfishness, or bitterness toward your spouse: a pig in the Holy of Holies. Sleeping around casually because that's the way to know if you're "truly compatible" with someone else: a pig and a statue of Zeus in the Holy of Holies, your own and the other person's heart and spirit as well as body.

"For as he thinks in his heart, so is he" (Proverbs 23:7, NKJV).

I need to learn to regard everyone I see as a repository for the image of God, every heart as a holy place, but I must reserve the holy of holies in my heart and body for the holy of holies in only one other vessel, exclusively. One sacred space, one place of consecration, held apart, honoring the God who created this place for two to meet with Him as one, out of honor for the Spirit in us each and both.

Are you bringing pigs of any sort into your temple? Your body and your thoughts are holy, sacred spaces. Cleanse the altar, dedicate yourself to God, keep your sacred space sacred, and hold it as consecrated until you enter the sacred space of lifelong covenant. If you are in covenant, keep your covenant emotionally, spiritually, and physically.

A "but" to pray: Oh, holy and righteous God, You created my body, my heart, my mind and spirit to be a vessel for Your Spirit, sanctified, holy and set apart for You through Jesus, first of all. Show me where I may have brought pigs into my temple by _____. Show me where I may have desecrated my husband/wife by bringing _____ into our union. Help me/us to consecrate this part of our lives again to You, give us joy in the holiness, and help us to _____

_____

_ to honor You, Holy Spirit, in the center of our union. In Jesus's name, amen! Holy Spirit, I'm listening.

_____

Sandwich Hugs

Children speak so eloquently straight from the Spirit. Smelling the cinnamon rolls my older son was baking for breakfast, I showered and dressed for church on Mother's Day morning at his house. From the master bedroom, I heard my six-year-old granddaughter's invitation, "Grandma, come and cuddle!" She'd spent the night in the big king-size bed with her daddy and mommy so I could sleep in her bed overnight, and that's where I found her curled up against my daughter-in-law.

Dressed or not, how could I refuse such a wonderful request? I crawled under the sheet and snuggled up next to Elsa for a big hug.

"Hey, we're making an Elsa sandwich," I laughed. Elsa is well acquainted with sandwich hugs, securely squished between daddy and mommy, and often with her brother Evan as part of the "filling." Sandwich hugs were part of our family ritual on weekends when my boys were growing up, too.

On guided tours, night camps, and during summer camps, when I worked at the zoo, we always made "instructor sandwiches" to keep the groups of children safe between us adults, so no one got lost. I told the children they were the peanut butter, jelly, lettuce, tomatoes, cheese, pickles, salami, onions, olives, mustard, mayonnaise—whatever they wanted to be, and they always called out plenty of disgusting combinations to make things fun. I enjoyed encouraging them because it built camaraderie between us. No, we didn't bunch up into one big hug, and granted, the "filling" tended to ooze out the sides, but we never lost a camper when they stayed between us.

I asked Elsa what kind of filling she was, and she replied, "Cream cheese." We put our heads together, literally, and tried to decide what Evan might be. "Jelly? Or bologna [or rather, baloney]?" I joked. We tried to figure out how to fit the entire family into one sandwich hug and decided the best "bread" to be between is God our Father and Jesus the Bread of Life.

"One day, we all *will* be!" I offered. "Hmm, but what about the Holy Spirit? Are we a triple-decker sandwich?"

"Oh, he'll be sprinkled on top of us like poppy seeds," Elsa smiled, "or like olive oil!"

What a hug that will make with the oil of the Holy Spirit poured out on us! And yes, I do believe in a God so intimately loving as Father that He probably can't wait to have us all safely in His arms. I suspect that's where we are in this life, too, when we make Him our Father, whether we feel it or not.

"Let the beloved of the LORD rest secure in him, for he shields him all day long, and the one the LORD loves rests between his shoulders" (Deuteronomy 33:12).

> Then Jesus declared, "I am the bread of life. He who comes to me will never go hungry, and he who believes in me will never be thirsty [...] All that the Father gives me will come to me, and whoever comes to me I will never drive away. For I have come down from heaven not to do my will but to do the will of him who sent me. And this is the will of him who sent me, that I shall lose none of all that he has given me, but raise them up at the last day."
>
> John 6:35-39

> Because I live, you also will live. On that day you will realize that I am in my Father, and you are in me, and I am in you [...] He who loves me will be loved by my Father, and I too will love him and show myself to him.
>
> John 14:20-21

Did I feel lonely since I lost the man I loved? Yes, of course, painfully so sometimes, and I longed for arms to wrap me again securely in faithful love. *But* God's presence has always been here for me. Out of His love, God brought me a new pair of arms and a heart that loves Jesus and honors me. Even so, I always will believe the one most present and most real with me is the One who reminds me, "The one the LORD loves rests between his shoulders." God doesn't want any of us lost.

I call that a hug to be cherished, don't you?

Six-year-old arms are pretty wonderful, too: "Grandma, you and Mommy are blueberry bagels today."

A "but" to pray: God, I feel so alone sometimes. Even in the middle of a crowd, and even in the middle of my family, still I long to truly feel Your arms around me. I want all my family with me in that hug, *but* no matter how far they are or how far I feel from You, I'll let You be the bread of life and dare to believe that You want to __

_____

_____. Scandalous intimacy, I know, but a scandalous love wraps me in an eternal sandwich hug! In Jesus's name, amen. Holy Spirit, I'm listening.

_____

Leapin' Lizards

I could have pretended when the lizard ran across the trail in front of me. I was walking with a man, and I could have clutched his shoulder, turned my head into his chest, and squealed, "Oh, [_____] [he shall remain nameless], a *lizard*! I'm so scared! Throw a rock at it! Make it go away!" And after he did, I'd look up into his eyes, bat mine, and in a higher voice than I use to speak with my female friends, I'd swooningly say, "Oh [_____], you're so brave and strong!" And if he took the bait...I'd be calling that man to a level lower than his true courage, integrity, and valor. Pardon me saying this, but *puke*! In spiritual terms, that translates to "abomination."

I've seen it, ladies. I've listened as you did it, and even if you are truly afraid of lizards, do you think falsely building up, or rather, buttering up, a man's ego calls him to greatness? It may salve his insecurity, but Jesus wants more for him and from him than a false hero status. God wants him to live in greatness. Guys, would you give that woman a second and third look and then tell her that her husband wants to be praised for true courage? Add that God wants her to live in greatness.

"A man who flatters his neighbor spreads a net for his feet" (Proverbs 29:5, ESV).

"For there is no truth in their mouth; their inmost self is destruction; their throat is an open grave; they flatter with their tongue" (Psalm 5:9, ESV).

"Faithful are the wounds of a friend; profuse are the kisses of an enemy" (Proverbs 27:6, ESV).

"For such persons do not serve our Lord Christ, but their own appetites, and by smooth talk and flattery they deceive the hearts of the naive" (Romans 16:18, ESV).

Gentlemen, I'm addressing this to you, and ladies, to you as well. Let us speak the truth to each other in love, true admiration where it's merited, true admonition when it's needed.

The lizard ran across the trail in front of me, and instead of shrieking—gosh, it was just a small, striped lizard, terrified of my big feet clumping down the trail close to its tail—I gave a very fake shriek, feigned terror (after having told my companion I like lizards) and then in all seriousness said, "[_____], if you want to show me how courageous you really are, if you want to make this Christian girl swoon, load a 'mortar round' of prayer and lob it at the devil for me!" That is courage! *That* is a true hero! God's grace to propel into greatness!

And I wasn't kidding. This friend has fasted for me and prayed for me, and if I truly care about him as a friend and brother in Christ, my job is to call forth the greatness in him, the greatest greatness he can live. I can't encourage him in sin, no matter how tempting it might be to lead him into a false sense of superhuman stature just to get his affection. The math teacher in me, I'd be degrading him to the "lowest common (cultural) denominator." Oh, gag, how insulting I would be if I even thought of encouraging a brother to sin, and how denigrating I would be if I didn't believe in the greatness Jesus has instilled in him through the Holy Spirit to call him to courageous action, to the "greatest uncommon denominator" of the best, truest, and most courageous life God has for him, conforming to the likeness of Jesus as a blood-bought child of God. "My agenda" for him means nothing; God's agenda for him means everything. GUCD!

I acknowledge here that I did do something for a loved one that allowed him to think the sin he was in, by his own words, "Wasn't so bad, and if that's the worst of [my] sins, well, God made me this way." Oh, the vile lie of the devil! Did I think I was being submissive to enable him to sin without consequences or speaking to him that he, that his integrity, was worth more than that? Was my compliance being obedient and submissive, or was it allowing him to stay at a level far below the true courage, integrity, honor, dignity, purity, and valor God intended that man to live in and live out? I don't take responsibility for his sin, but I am responsible for how I responded to it. Suppose I'd had the courage to trust God enough to speak up out of loving truth and called him to righteousness in his choices. God would have taken care of me no matter what his response was, as long as my motives were for his best, for his true grace-given greatness.

As I relate to others now years later, I recognize that I cannot call forth less than the greatest from my brothers and sisters. When I consider the price God paid for her, for him, when I think of the treasure that person is to God's heart, how can I use, manipulate, or hold her or him to less than the most meaningful, vital, alive, on-fire life from all God's spirit has poured into them, to live in and live out of them?

> See what great love the Father has lavished on us, that we should be called children of God! And that is what we are! The reason the world does not know us is that it did not know him. Dear friends, now we are children of God, and what we will be has not yet been made known. But we know that when Christ

appears, we shall be like him, for we shall see him as he is. All who have this hope in him purify themselves, just as he is pure. Everyone who sins breaks the law; in fact, sin is lawlessness. But you know that he appeared so that he might take away our sins. And in him is no sin. No one who lives in him keeps on sinning. No one who continues to sin has either seen him or known him.

Dear children, do not let anyone lead you astray. The one who does what is right is righteous, just as he is righteous. The one who does what is sinful is of the devil, because the devil has been sinning from the beginning. The reason the Son of God appeared was to destroy the devil's work. No one who is born of God will continue to sin, because God's seed remains in them; they cannot go on sinning, because they have been born of God. This is how we know who the children of God are and who the children of the devil are: Anyone who does not do what is right is not God's child, nor is anyone who does not love their brother and sister.

1 John 3:1-10

I love the hymn "How Deep the Father's Love" by Stuart Townend. Knowing the price God paid in watching His beloved suffer whipping and then the indignity and agony of the cross, how can we think God means for grace to do anything less than call us to greatness, true greatness? Ought we to do less, ought we to lower our expectations of each other and give flattery instead of encouragement to greatness? Why would I want to allow someone I love to live in anything less than the grace and greatness God gifted her or him with when she or he made Jesus their Lord? If Jesus is his Lord, her Lord, then he is a son of the King of Kings, and she is a daughter of the Lord of All, grace gifted through Jesus to rise in strength, courage, compassion, valor, dignity, kindness, purity and truth to live a life and leave a legacy of greatness.

> How deep the Father's love for us,
> How vast beyond all measure,
> That He should give His only Son
> To make a wretch His treasure.[8]

My stand cost me dearly because I couldn't let a loved one live out less than the greatness God his Father called him to. Others, "friends" and colleagues, spoke into his life to encourage him to conform to the standards of the world and live far below the integrity

God wanted him to live in and live out. Is encouraging someone to live in the lowest common cultural denominator true love?

I purpose, and I pray you may consider calling the people you love in your life to the truest greatness they can live in and live out. A measure of our love is the measure of grace-gifted greatness we call forth in and from each other.

> Behold what manner of love the Father has bestowed on us, that we should be called children of God! Therefore the world does not know us, because it did not know Him. Beloved, now we are children of God; and it has not yet been revealed what we shall be, but we know that when He is revealed, we shall be like Him, for we shall see Him as He is. And everyone who has this hope in Him purifies himself, just as He is pure.
>
> 1 John 3:1-3 (NKJV)

Verse two of the song is this proclamation:

> I will not boast in anything,
> No gifts, no power, no wisdom;
> But I will boast in Jesus Christ
> His death and resurrection.

Why should I gain from His reward?
I cannot give an answer;
But this I know with all my heart—
His wounds have paid my ransom.[9]

So then, what does this ask of us? All I want to do is
be a soul on fire for the love and purity of God and call it
forth in the hearts of others! So, my sisters, my friends,
my brothers, lob a grenade of prayer at the enemy in the
lives of those you love today! Selah! Amen!

A "but" to pray: God, I've settled for less than courage in my own life. I've even tantalized others to live in
so much less than the greatness of Your grace in them
to flatter them and make them like me or to "get" something from them, but today I purpose to, and ask You
to help me to call _____ to the best in ____

_____

that You long for him/her! I want to be a God pleaser,
not a people pleaser. I truly do want to raise the bar in
our culture and challenge myself first to rethink how I
live in less than my truest self _____
_____, then challenge the people I love to live
up to *Your* standards in _____
_____. Show me who needs
this kind of love from me _____
_____ and, Holy Spirit, give me true
wisdom and insight to know how, when, and where to

speak, what to say, and when I should keep my counsel if words won't be the best strategy. Give me strategies to truly build others up to their highest self. In Jesus's name, amen. Holy Spirit, I'm listening.

Freedom for Responsibility

If we're honest, probably most of us long for the job, or the time, or the money to allow us to be free *from* responsibility. That's part of the appeal of retirement and financial independence: no accountability to anyone but ourselves for nothing but pleasurable purposes.

How long, I wonder, would that lifestyle provide meaning and satisfaction to us? If today I could go anywhere I wanted, do anything I wanted to do, eat whatever I wanted, buy whatever I wanted, would I feel validated as a person? Isn't that what that kind of "freedom" means when we examine our motives in wanting it?

If what I truly long for is validation, a sense that my life matters and has meaning, then I look to the cross of Jesus, the sacrifice that set us free from the Mosaic law, keeping an interminable set of rules, constantly failing in some point, and feeling the sting of knowing we didn't "measure up." Performance: we look for it in cars, from each other on the job, and sadly from each other in a relationship. "I will love you *if* you...*when* you...*because* you..."

Grace turns that kind of thinking radically on its head, where it belongs, swept away from our lives, thoughts, actions, and relationships because of the immeasurable grace God gives us daily in the death of His Son Jesus on the cross in our places.

"What do You mean, God, I can't do anything to earn Your grace? What do You mean that I can't possibly measure up? That means I have to *admit* that I can't measure up, and that makes me invalidated, worthless...doesn't it?"

No, it means exactly the opposite: each of us has immeasurable value to God just because He wants us in a relationship with Him. How in the universe can that be? Because He is love, period.

> But now apart from the law the righteousness of God has been made known, to which the Law and the Prophets testify. This righteousness is given through faith in Jesus Christ to all who believe. There is no difference between Jew and Gentile, for all have sinned and fall short of the glory of God, and all are

justified freely by his grace through the redemption that came by Christ Jesus.

Romans 3:21-24

For through the law I died to the law so that I
might live for God. I have been crucified with
Christ and I no longer live, but Christ lives
in me. The life I now live in the body, I live
by faith in the Son of God, who loved me and
gave himself for me.

Galatians 2:19-20

Speak and act as those who are going to be
judged by the law that gives freedom, because judgment without mercy will be shown
to anyone who has not been merciful. Mercy
triumphs over judgment.

James 2:12-13

Responding to that merciful love means I want to
show it, return some measure of my limited love to
that limitless love. I want to give! Love is the illogic that
stands logic on its ugly head and liberates everyone
who embraces it to *freely* give, to take on responsibility
with a joyful, willing heart.

"Heal the sick, raise the dead, cleanse those who have
leprosy, drive out demons. Freely you have received;
freely give" (Matthew 10:8).

My neighbor was living on rice and beans, and I had the ability to buy a package of chicken at 50 percent off the usual price. Was I legally responsible for my neighbor? No, but out of love, could I say she was loved in a tangible way? Yes, freely.

> This is how we know what love is: Jesus Christ laid down his life for us. And we ought to lay down our lives for our brothers and sisters. If anyone has material possessions and sees a brother or sister in need but has no pity on them, how can the love of God be in that person? Dear children, let us not love with words or speech but with actions and in truth.
>
> 1 John 3:16-18

At a fund-raising yard sale at my church, a woman admired a red two-piece suit I had for sale. She couldn't afford the yard sale price. Did I owe it to her to give it to her? *No*, but did God's *grace*, God's riches at Christ's expense, give me the freedom to give away something I could give to bless the heart of someone else? Yes, and to joyfully put the $5.00 in the mission fund myself! Wow, she was going to feel beautiful in that suit!

I hurt someone's feelings. But God, they hurt me, too. If I apologize—no, if I say the dreaded three words, "I was *wrong*,"—won't that diminish my value? Won't that make *me* wrong, mean I failed, and I lose my worth?

No—grace gives me the freedom to admit I was wrong, knowing the person I hurt is immeasurably valued by God, and so am I! He wants the right relationships for our mutual good.

Freedom to *be* responsible, freedom *for* responsibility toward God and toward others.

> Therefore, there is now no condemnation for those who are in Christ Jesus, because through Christ Jesus the law of the Spirit who gives life has set you free from the law of sin and death. For what the law was powerless to do because it was weakened by the flesh, God did by sending his own Son in the likeness of sinful flesh to be a sin offering. And so he condemned sin in the flesh, in order that the righteous requirement of the law might be fully met in us, who do not live according to the flesh but according to the Spirit. Those who live according to the flesh have their minds set on what the flesh desires; but those who live in accordance with the Spirit have their minds set on what the Spirit desires.
>
> Romans 8:1-5

> In the same way, count yourselves dead to sin but alive to God in Christ Jesus. Therefore do not let sin reign in your mortal body so that

you obey its evil desires. Do not offer any part of yourself to sin as an instrument of wickedness, but rather offer yourselves to God as those who have been brought from death to life; and offer every part of yourself to him as an instrument of righteousness. For sin shall no longer be your master, because you are not under the law, but under grace.

What then? Shall we sin because we are not under the law but under grace? By no means! Don't you know that when you offer yourselves to someone as obedient slaves, you are slaves of the one you obey—whether you are slaves to sin, which leads to death, or to obedience, which leads to righteousness? But thanks be to God that, though you used to be slaves to sin, you have come to obey from your heart the pattern of teaching that has now claimed your allegiance. You have been set free from sin and have become slaves to righteousness.

I am using an example from everyday life because of your human limitations. Just as you used to offer yourselves as slaves to impurity and to ever-increasing wickedness, so now offer yourselves as slaves to righteousness leading to holiness. When you were slaves to sin, you were free from the control of righteousness. What benefit did you reap at that time from the things you are now ashamed of? Those things result in death! But now that you have been set free from sin and have become slaves of God, the benefit you reap leads to holiness, and the result is eternal life.

Romans 6:11-22

As the song says, I am free to love, I am free to dance, I am free to live for *You*, I am free!

A "but" to pray: Oh, God, Your mercy for me, Your unmerited favor You lavished on me through the gift of Your Son Jesus given freely for me to bring me into a family relationship with You as Your child and friend gives me the heart to be glad to return Your love in serving. I admit I've lived for myself and my own pleasures in _____ and frankly, that never gave me the value and worth that living freely *in* Your love to *give* Your love gives to me. Show me who needs Your love today as I _____ and give me the courage of love to _____ _____. In the name of the awesome lover of my soul, Jesus, *amen*! Holy Spirit, I'm listening.

Exactly What We Needed

I gasped and blinked back tears, hardly believing what I saw. For the second time in four months, the sight ahead of me stopped me in my tracks.

First had been the sight of my husband walking down the sidewalk to meet me, briefcase in hand, in the middle of the day: a picture forever etched in my memory. It was the day the Gulf War began and the day the life we'd known ended. A friend had come up to my husband at work that morning and told him to clear out his desk. Small comfort that my husband was one of the last laid off as his company downsized from 2,500 to just 500 employees. His job loss at this date meant hundreds of engineers had already filled any openings in local companies. We both shrugged that thought aside, certain that my husband's abilities and God's guidance would connect him with another job in a short time.

And that's exactly what happened—almost—when another aerospace firm offered him a job just four weeks later, in exactly the kind of project he'd been working on, for a foreign customer. We rejoiced because this company was close to our church, and we envisioned a new house in a new neighborhood, and our long Sunday commute whittled down to a few minutes. That was Friday. On Monday, my husband was scheduled to settle on a salary and sign all the paperwork, but the new boss called instead to say, "The government pushed the contract back. Could you wait six months to start work?" Six months for what might never materialize at all? Our elation evaporated, leaving a vacuum, quickly filled with confusion and questions without answers, not the least of which was my wounded cry, "God, why? Why put something so perfect in our reach and then take it away? Don't You care about us?"

"Between unemployment and our savings, we can make it through the summer," my husband quietly advised me, "but we'll have to cut out everything nonessential from our budget." We gritted our teeth, retrenched our hearts, and set our minds to eliminating as many expenses as we could. That meant I sewed shorts for our rapidly growing teenage son. If it embarrassed him to wear homemade clothing, he graciously never said so. It also meant our entertainment now became borrowing videos from the public library rather than even going to the dollar movie theater. We tried to make a game of finding free or inexpensive new options to replace our old activities, intentionally putting a positive spin on our circumstances and conversations for the sake of our two children. My husband and I were both concerned as we watched our savings dwindle week by week, but the last thing we wanted was to pass our anxiety along to the boys. Weeks turned into months as my husband networked, searched, and mailed resumes, diligently looking for work, with not even one interview to show for all his perseverance. I substitute taught as often as I could, but that meant many days when my husband had to stay home with our four-year-old son, days he couldn't devote to job hunting.

Any vacation was out of the question, so when my sister called to ask if we'd like to go boating with them at the lake for the weekend, I joyfully and thankfully shot back, "Sure thing!" Excitedly I began checking off things we'd need: "Sleeping bags, check; fishing poles, check; bathing suits, check..." A sudden realization sank my anticipation like an anchor tossed overboard. Damming rivers forms most lakes in Arizona and fills canyons with water, so our lakes don't have sandy beaches. Instead, the shallows are covered with sharp rocks, so you have to wear shoes to go swimming. Our younger son only had two pairs of shoes: one dress pair and one good pair of tennis shoes. We couldn't afford him to ruin either pair, but we also couldn't afford to buy another pair of even cheap shoes for him. The last thing I wanted to do was cancel the trip and sink our sons' happiness at finally doing something resembling our old "normal" life, so I asked my husband, "Could we stop by the thrift store on our way to the lake on Saturday?" I had exactly one dollar to spend, but I felt cautiously optimistic that I could find an old pair of children's tennis shoes that might come close to fitting our son, so we piled our gear into the car that Saturday morning, relishing the eager "on our way" chatter from the back seat.

I leaped out of the car at the thrift store, praying, and dashed into the shop. That's when I stopped short at what sat on a display rack directly in front of me. Almost afraid to look, I turned over the brand new pair of blue "water socks," still sporting their original price tag, to look for a size. They were exactly the size our son wore, and they were exactly one dollar.

"And my God will supply all your needs according to His riches in glory in Christ Jesus. Now to our God and Father be the glory forever and ever. Amen" (Philippians 4:19-20, NASB).

> Do not be anxious about anything, but in every situation, by prayer and petition, with thanksgiving, present your requests to God.

And the peace of God, which transcends all understanding, will guard your hearts and your minds in Christ Jesus.

Philippians 4:6-7

Can any one of you by worrying add a single hour to your life? And why do you worry about clothes? See how the flowers of the field grow. They do not labor or spin. Yet I tell you that not even Solomon in all his splendor was dressed like one of these. If that is how God clothes the grass of the field, which is here today and tomorrow is thrown into the fire, will he not much more clothe you—you of little faith? So do not worry, saying, "What shall we eat?" or "What shall we drink?" or "What shall we wear?" For the pagans run after all these things, and your heavenly Father knows that you need them. But seek first his kingdom and his righteousness, and all these things will be given to you as well.

Matthew 6:27-33

Many people would consider this a minor coincidence. To me, it was a major miracle and a sign from a faithful God that He did care and had "plans to prosper you and not to harm you, plans to give you hope and a future" (Jeremiah 29:11). As we drove on, one elated four-year-old in the back seat happily trying on his glorious new shoes, I pondered all the "coincidences" that had to come together to create this small piece of providence:

- Someone had to buy the shoes in exactly our son's size.
- Those shoes had to be unsuitable for some reason.
- The purchaser had to choose to donate rather than return the shoes to the store.
- The purchaser had to donate the shoes to that particular organization.
- The shoes had to make their way to that organization's particular small thrift store in our neighborhood.
- They had to come in at exactly the time we needed to find a pair of shoes.
- They had to be marked for exactly what I could afford to spend.
- No one else could have spotted and bought them before me.
- I had to decide to stop at that particular thrift store, on just the right day, at exactly the right time.

At least nine coincidences had to converge to create this "ordinary" yet exactly perfect provision for us. What we found was more than just a pair of shoes! Though the shoes were exactly what—and even better than—we needed, what we needed most of all was hope: tangible, clear evidence to me that God knew and cared about our needs. My wounded faith was healed at that moment, my heart dared to hope again, and I knew somehow our family would be okay.

It was two more months until my husband found a job, the week his unemployment benefits ran out. In yet another "ordinary" miracle, he applied for an assembly line position but was hired as an engineer for an opening the company hadn't even advertised.

God proved Himself for my son and his family, too, in a difficult time in their lives. Working in Asia on support, they had to raise themselves; one month, their supply was so limited that they had to choose between buying diapers for their daughter or buying food. Choosing food as the greater need, they went home trusting God to help them manage somehow. Sitting on their doorstep was a wrapped birthday gift from friends for their daughter: you guessed it, a box of diapers!

> Ask, and it will be given to you; seek, and you
> will find; knock, and it will be opened to you.
> For everyone who asks receives, and the one
> who seeks finds, and to the one who knocks it

will be opened. Or which one of you, if his son asks him for bread, will give him a stone? Or if he asks for a fish, will give him a serpent? If you then, who are evil, know how to give good gifts to your children, how much more will your Father who is in heaven give good things to those who ask him!

Matthew 7:7-11 (ESV)

Those blue water socks have been a "boat ramp" to launch my hope and confidence in God in many turbulent waters since then. Even in the receding waters of national financial recession, those two blue shoes still reassure me that God knows, God cares, and God will still fashion coincidence upon coincidence to create "ordinary" miracles that exactly meet our needs!

And He has said to me, "My grace is sufficient for you, for power is perfected in weakness." Most gladly, therefore, I will rather boast about my weaknesses, so that the power of Christ may dwell in me. Therefore I am well content with weaknesses, with insults, with distresses, with persecutions, with difficulties, for Christ's sake; for when I am weak, then I am strong.

2 Corinthians 12:9-10 (NASB)

A "but" to pray: almighty Father, you are Jehovah Jireh, my Provider, You promise me that Your grace is sufficient to supply all my needs. It's hard to believe when _____, *but* You mean what You say in Your Word. Trusting in Your love for me and trusting in Your goodness, I lift up my deepest need to You today to supply in my life according to Your grace and power _____

_____

_____.

Surprise me, God, good heavenly Father, with the blessing You choose, in the way You choose, and in the time You choose; I *do* believe You still delight in working miracles, so here is my need for Your glory: _____

_____

_____. In Jesus's name, amen! Holy Spirit, I'm listening.

_____

Motown Jesus: Everlasting Love

In 1967, Robert Knight recorded a song written by Mac Gayden, lyrics by Buzz Cason. For those not born in the United States: within the 1940s through 1960s, Detroit, Michigan, was noted for two products: automobiles and music, gaining it the label of "Motor City" and the rock and blues music that came from Detroit "Motown." I've loved their song ever since I first heard it. Teenage girls could weep thinking of finding a love like this song proclaimed. Then some of us discovered that the Prince Charming who found us was really just another wounded human being searching for but unable to give the same thing we were searching for and longing to be part of, the song's name: "Everlasting Love."

Buzz Cayson said he was inspired by the words of Jeremiah 31:3-4: "The LORD appeared to us in the past, saying: 'I have loved you with an everlasting love; I have drawn you with unfailing kindness [...] Again you will take up your tambourines and go out to dance with the joyful.'"

Aha! I always thought I heard God speaking in that song! Something in it called to me when I was just seventeen and lodged deeply in my heart. I knew Jesus because I grew up in a church-going, God-loving family, but my knowledge became full-blown love in our tiny church on February 20, 1972, when I "heard" Jesus say to me, "You know I died for the world...but do you know I died for *you*?"

Wow! Chosen! Beloved! I was going to need that deepest love inside me to carry me through the shattering of my world decades later. Rock-solid, Jesus's love for me, passionate and burning, tender and embracing. Why do we demand from each other the unconditional love that only our Father Creator God can give us through Himself made flesh and blood in Jesus? "Hearts go astray, leaving hurt when they go..." Our hearts get wounded; we close them up to keep from bleeding or keep the world from seeing our bleeding and the depth of our need. Being "needy" isn't cool, but in reality, we all are. Wounded animals conceal their pain and vulnerability so predators won't single them out for a meal. I suspect we humans do the same thing.

"Nobody is going to ever talk like *that* to me again!"

"I won't let anyone treat me like *that* again!"

"No, I'm fine, really, I'm picking myself up and moving on..." and so we go, bleeding all the way. We close off our hearts from the ones who have hurt us, but brick by brick, does that wall keep out the very love we need, and does it keep out the love Jesus may send to us through others?

If it's true that "you can't heal what you don't reveal," it may also be very true that you can't heal what you don't let yourself feel, or more accurately, how can Jesus heal what we aren't willing to feel? Feeling hurts, we feel because we care, and the ones we care about the most are the ones whose wounds hurt us most deeply. The truth hidden there is that we/I/*you* hurt because we/I/*you do* have a heart capable of knowing and wanting love, empathy, a consciousness of and conscience toward the feelings of others, and we expect others to be wired as we are. Sadly, tragically, not every person is, *but* amazingly, incredibly, *Jesus is!*

Whatever else happens to us in this life amid the wounded, predator, prey, and innocent bystanders minding their own business and trying to live uprightly, we do well to remember we "wrestle not against flesh and blood."

> For our struggle is not against flesh and blood, but against the rulers, against the authorities, against the powers of this dark

world and against the spiritual forces of evil
in the heavenly realms. Therefore put on the
full armor of God, so that when the day of evil
comes, you may be able to stand your ground,
and after you have done everything, to stand.

Ephesians 6:12-13

Paul goes on to describe the helmet of faith, the
breastplate of salvation, the belt of truth, the shoes of
the readiness to preach the gospel, and the sword of
God's Word. That brings me back full circle to Isaiah
31:3 and the promise God can't possibly break: that He
loves us/me/you with an everlasting love and draws us
to Himself with kindness. Can I dare, can you dare, to
open up your heart and feel that you're part of everlasting love? Can we wear that love like chain mail to protect our hearts without walling them off from the lives
around us who can, at best, love us despite our, and
through their, limitations?

I know this: I can only approach feeling and living
out unconditional love for others when I let Jesus into
my heart to heal what's out of tune within me and then
to love others through me, even while I'm healing. The
Motown song implies we can find this love in other
people, but it's truly only God's love for us through Jesus's love that is and enables everlasting love.

Unlike in the lyrics, Jesus never will leave us:

For He [God] Himself has said, I will not in any way fail you nor give you up nor leave you without support. [I will] not, [I will] not, [I will] not in any degree leave you helpless nor forsake nor let [you] down (relax My hold on you)! [Assuredly not!]

Hebrews 13:5 (AMPCE);
brackets and parentheses in the original

Jesus promised to embrace everyone who comes to Him with an everlasting love:

All those the Father gives me will come to me, and whoever comes to me I will never drive away. For I have come down from heaven not to do my will but to do the will of him who sent me. And this is the will of him who sent me that I shall lose none of all those he has given me, but raise them up at the last day.

John 6:37-39

Had Motown been around in those days, Jesus might have sung it rather than said it. Can you hear His call to you in this song? More importantly, can you hear the voice of "Motown" Jesus calling to you in His song for you today? Listen to it online, and as you listen, write down the words that God's spirit speaks to you, about you, in the song "Everlasting Love," written by Buzz Cason and Mac Gayden, originally a 1967 hit for Robert Knight.

A "but" to pray: Jesus, I'm going to be very honest. I need Your healing touch and everlasting love. It's true that I've _____
___, and it's true that _____
____ said _____
_____ to me. It's true that _____
did _____
__ to me, and if I'm really honest, it's true that I said
_____
and I did _____
_____, and I wish I hadn't let my "heart go astray" from forgiving and understanding. I could easily wall off my heart, *but* Father God, You love me with an everlasting love that I don't have to come back with regret beggin' for! You said it, You promise it, You mean it, and so I will let You come into my heart. Help my unbelief, keep my heart from going astray from Yours, and help me feel Your everlasting love. Can I dance with You to this song today, and when I do, please help me feel You with me. In Jesus's name, amen. Holy Spirit, I'm listening.

_____

I Want (to Be Like) Candy

This title comes from an old song by the Strange-loves, released in 1965, called "I Want Candy."

I know—and I was challenged and changed by—a woman named Candy. Nobody would give her a second look. Yes, she has long flowing hair, but there her resemblance to the girl on the beach in 1965 ends. Strangely enough, I know this Candy is infinitely more beautiful than the Candy of the Bo Diddley beat, and if I could have a heart half as caring and kind as hers, I'd be glad because Candy's selfless, self-giving love humbles me.

I met her one morning at church in our women's ministry: long hair stringing straight down, carrying extra pounds, some teeth broken, wearing glasses, shorter than my 5'5", not well-educated, completely ingenious and genuine, from somewhere around the hills of West Virginia, a woman who used the phrase "I might could..." betraying her humble roots. There I was, the morning speaker for the message, table discussion leader, former National Merit Scholar, blessed with a good education, born in the Midwest where yes, my extended family used the term "red up" to mean "clean the table," but I'd never said that in my life. Candy was the kind of person that some shy away from in order to not be considered as simple and "uncool" as she. What did we have in common? We shared wearing glasses, and we shared loving Jesus. I might have been delivering the morning message, but I had a lot to learn from Candy.

We'd talk when we met in the lobby at church, but I never called her or went to lunch with her. Some days, she needed a ride to the women's meetings, and I'd pick her up and return her home. There I was, doing my "good Christian duty." Oh, was I about to be set straight! Candy volunteered with the "friendship class" at our church, a Sunday school class for the developmentally disabled, including quite a few adults with Down's syndrome. She loved those people with such respect and compassion that I began to marvel at the heart of this woman.

Candy talked with real admiration about comments some of the class members made on Sunday mornings. She was always ready to serve in women's ministry, too, helping set and clear tables, giving hugs to anyone who would accept one. She beamed when she and the other class leaders led the friendship class onto the stage at church to sing in our Sunday morning services. They always got a standing ovation! Some Sundays, they put on skits, and there was hardly a dry eye in the house. Several of those childlike young people also helped usher on Sunday mornings, and why not? Weren't they fully vested Christians too? Didn't they merit a chance to use their gifts to serve? Didn't Jesus count them worthy of shedding His blood and enduring the whip and the cross that they could know how deeply, desperately, relentlessly God loves them?

Candy cried with me when my husband left me, and the rug got pulled out from under all I'd cherished and believed with no recrimination, no condemnation, no "what didn't you do right?" She simply loved from that genuine, kind, simply good, simply Christlike heart of hers, and I was grateful. I needed her friendship more than she ever needed a car ride from me.

> But the LORD said to Samuel, "Do not consider his appearance or his height, for I have rejected him. The LORD does not look at the things people look at. People look at the outward appearance, but the LORD looks at the heart."
>
> 1 Samuel 16:7

Brothers and sisters, think of what you were when you were called. Not many of you were wise by human standards; not many were influential; not many were of noble birth. But God chose the foolish things of the world to shame the wise; God chose the weak things of the world to shame the strong. God chose the lowly things of this world and the despised things—and the things that are not—to nullify the things that are, so that no one may boast before him. It is because of him that you are in Christ Jesus, who has become for us wisdom from God—that is, our righteousness, holiness and redemption. Therefore, as it is written: "Let the one who boasts boast in the Lord."

1 Corinthians 1:26-31

So, rightly humbled and blessed and honored to call her my friend, I want (to be like) Candy, a woman softhearted and sweet, fine as gold refined in the fire with a heart few others could claim to approximate. Yes, Candy does have something I desire very much: to love with the selfless, caring, joyfully appreciating, and others-validating heart of Jesus. Candy, I respect, honor, admire, and love you, my teacher and my friend!

A "but" to pray: God, I am so quick to judge and compare people based on outward appearances or superficial qualities before I even take a few minutes to see who they are in character and heart. Help me, Father, to see the good in _____ today and give me an opportunity to tell _____ how much I value him/her. Keep my eyes open for others who need to know how truly wonderful they are, and give me eyes to see below the surface and honor as You do what You've placed inside them. And Lord, when I feel I don't measure up to the standards others set for me, help me be gracious and remember that You dance over me with singing (Zephaniah 3:17). In Jesus's name, amen. Holy Spirit, I'm listening.

Tandem: New Rules for the Road

Gosh, I can hear the Bible as I'm riding, I thought as I pushed a little faster than I wanted to and shot down the hill on two thin tires at thirty-eight miles per hour, keenly aware there was nothing between my skin and the asphalt but a thin jersey and bike shorts. Others must surely have seen the same parallels riding on the back of a tandem road bike; now, I entered their cadre, not entirely willingly. I ride with a man who loves cycling. Before I met him, I enjoyed riding my bike to the grocery store and back and noodling around the neighborhood on evening pleasure rides. He, however, is of the "conquer the hills, the faster, the better" squadron, and he knows I'll love riding once I get more miles under me and build up my endurance. Humph.

I look at the hill he'd love to climb, at least an 8 percent grade all the twenty-mile way to the top of the mountain, and I shudder. I never want to be *that* fit!

When we ride independently, I usually "flake off" at the eight-mile mark, cut across a road lined seasonally with wildflowers and with a walking/biking path where I'll generally find someone to stop, say hello to, and pray with. The surprise of a perfect stranger offering to pray for them delights me. I am God's carrier pigeon on two wheels, bringing a word of His love to someone in their day, and I have fun being part of the "airdrops" He allows me to make.

I remember riding on the handlebars or on the back rack of my brother's bike. That was fun, and I didn't have to do any of the work!

But when I'm on the back of the tandem, new rules apply:

- Where he's going, I have to go. (And last week wearing his jersey and staring at his dorsal side, I wryly thought of how Peter must have felt when Jesus told him, "Very truly I tell you, when you were younger you dressed yourself and went where you wanted; but when you are old you will stretch out your hands, and someone else will dress you and lead you where you do not want to go," [John 21:18] and amen!)
- I can't see or control where we are going.
- As far as he goes, I have to go. (And I thought of the woman in the cycling club who replied to her husband's comment that she wasn't giving him

enough on the back of the bike, "If I give it all to you know, you aren't getting any of it when we get home!")

- I have to match his pedaling speed because I'm "clipped in." (Because against my protests, he did put clip pedals on and even bought me cycling shoes to lock into the clips so I can "give it more power" and use my hamstrings too. My hamstrings were quite happy letting my quads do the work, thank you very much, quit when they got tired, and I liked being able to freely leap off my bike if I started to fall.)
- Which brings me to this point: if he falls, I fall.
- When he stops, I stop. (Generally gratefully! At intersections, I counterbalance his foot on the ground.)
- I'm dependent upon his judgment, observation, care, and character.

These may sound like negatives, and in some ways, they are, but I choose to name them as "sobering realities."

He has a few "sobering realities" to face as well:

- He has to put his muscle to the pedals, but if I so choose, I can pretty much rest in his strength when I'm tired.

- I can take my hands off the handlebars and sit upright because he's steering.
- I can communicate my needs/limitations, and he will, out of consideration, choose an easier or shorter route (or face my stiff neck, sore wrists, and sat-out seat).
- When my energy is used up, it's up to him to get us home.
- If I shift my weight, he has to compensate to keep us upright. (Whew, I have to learn to reach for my water bottle without leaning to either side.)
- He is responsible for my safety.

I have heard the test of a relationship is if you can ride a tandem without killing each other. The rule is: what happens on the bike, stays on the bike. But every time I click my feet into those pedals, the word "captivity" springs to mind: the state or period of being held, imprisoned, enslaved, or confined. *But* that is one perspective, half of the truth. The other truth is that riding on the tandem makes a way for me to be with my friend and do what I couldn't do, without great exertion, on my own.

I also know this is true about a lasting relationship:

Perfect romantic love never does last, of course. Under the best conditions, it evolves into something more realistic and lasting, where two imperfect people discover one another's virtues and faults and grow to appreciate the goodness in each other—but also to accept the disappointments.[10]

I have to add, though I'd rather not: learn to accept challenges to grow, stretch, and get stronger.

As I crank my heart out grinding up the second or third of the "only one more hill" hills, I sometimes ruefully sing the old song to myself:

Daisy, Daisy, give me your answer, do.
I'm half-crazy all for the love of you.
It won't be a stylish marriage, I can't afford a carriage.
But you'll look sweet upon the seat of a bicycle built for two.

Words by Harry Dacre, 1892

The tandem truth is that, in sending Jesus, God made a way for us to receive what we can't do out of our own strength or "righteousness": ride with Him depending on His strength, endurance, blood, love.

A rabbi's disciples always walked in the dust of their teacher, following in his footsteps wherever he lead them. Jesus's disciples did the same, and if I want to be His disciple today, I'm going to have to put in some miles. I can't keep up with Him out of my own limited resources and "goodness," but I can clip into the pedals behind Him and ride where He's going. The disciples were on two feet; I'm on two feet with You, Jesus, and sometimes literally on two wheels in the company of some of Your competitive "conquer the mountain, harder, faster, longer, first" children who don't know You yet but need to. All I want to conquer is the enemy of my soul, not the pavement! Stop and smell the Texas sage, people! There are lonely folks to be prayed for out there...but they ride on. Sigh.

Okay. Once a week, at least, I saddle up as a sidekick. Hop on the back of the bike and lock in with Jesus, who genuinely is crazy about you and me, as you read these verses. Ask the Holy Spirit if and how they might apply to your life today:

"Let us hold fast the profession of our faith without wavering, for he who promised is faithful. And let us consider how we may spur one another on toward love and good deeds" (Hebrews 10:23-24).

> Through these he has given us his very great and precious promises, so that through them you may participate in the divine nature, having escaped the corruption in the world caused by evil desires.

For this very reason, make every effort to add to your faith goodness; and to goodness, knowledge; and to knowledge, self-control; and to self-control, perseverance; and to perseverance, godliness; and to godliness, mutual affection; and to mutual affection, love. For if you possess these qualities in increasing measure, they will keep you from being ineffective and unproductive in your knowledge of our Lord Jesus Christ.

2 Peter 1:4-8

Come to me, all you who are weary and burdened, and I will give you rest. Take my yoke upon you and learn from me, for I am gentle and humble in heart, and you will find rest for your souls. For my yoke is easy and my burden is light.

Matthew 11:28-30

"Since you are my rock and my fortress, for the sake of your name lead and guide me" (Psalm 31:3, emphasis mine).

"Then Jesus said to his disciples, 'Whoever wants to be my disciple must deny themselves and take up their cross and follow me'" (Matthew 16:24, emphasis mine).

"Whoever serves me must follow me; and where I am, my servant also will be. My Father will honor the one who serves me" (John 12:26, emphasis mine).

"Trust in the LORD with all your heart and lean not on your own understanding; in all your ways submit to him, and he will make your paths straight" (Proverbs 3:5-6a).

"*Two are better than one,* because they have a good return for their labor: If either of them falls down, one can help the other up" (Ecclesiastes 4:9-10, emphasis mine).

> Therefore if you have any encouragement from being united with Christ, if any comfort from his love, if any common sharing in the Spirit, if any tenderness and compassion, then make my joy complete by being like-minded, having the same love, being one in spirit and of one mind. Do nothing out of selfish ambition or vain conceit. Rather, in humility value others above yourselves, not looking to your own interests but each of you to the interests of the others.
>
> Philippians 2:1-4

> Do you not know? Have you not heard? The LORD is the everlasting God, the Creator of the ends of the earth.

He will not grow tired or weary, and his understanding no one can fathom. He gives strength to the weary and increases the power of the weak. Even youths grow tired and weary, and young men stumble and fall; but those who hope in the LORD will renew their strength. They will soar on wings like eagles; they will run and not grow weary, they will walk and not be faint.

Isaiah 40:28-31

Oh, God, that's what You want for me, isn't it? Rats! I'd much rather noodle around the neighborhood and never get serious about going somewhere with the faith and gifts and strengths You've given to and invested in me. I'd rather quit when I feel tired, hop off when I want, go where I want at the speed I want, and not be obligated to anyone for how long it takes me to get nowhere in particular. But I have a sneaking suspicion, and last week at a conference, I heard a "name" of God for the first time: "Jehovah Sneaky," that You want me to do something with the talents and desires and gifts You put in me, You want me to follow the road You planned for me, to go as far as You want to go, willingly stop when You stop, and trust Your love for me whether I can see where we're going or not. I recall speaking on this subject ten years ago, but then I hadn't been required to walk down a road I never wanted to travel for longer than I wanted to be in battle and in limbo. Now I've had to live it, and it hasn't been rainbows, bunnies, and flowers. It's been hard, uphill, in the dark, in the rain, against the wind, and a challenge to keep my heart free from bitterness, anger, pulling away from You, and fear every turn of the wheel.

God, You told me two things over two years ago: "You're worth fighting for" and "You are my chosen child. Don't be afraid of what man tries to do to you." You didn't tell me where we were going, how long the road would be, or how steep the climb. I suspect my fear and inability to hang on made this trip take longer and be harder than it needed to be. Did I switch places and try to be the one in front? Did I let go of the "manna" You gave me because I was grieving too hard? Well, I know You forgive me, and Your mercy is new every morning. I want to take the back seat now and let You pull me up the hill, pump hard when I can't, stop when I/we need to, and yes, I desperately need to trust Your character to take responsibility for my safety.

A "but" to pray: God, I know You want my life to count and have meaning. I do, too, but honestly, "clipping in" with You makes me feel _____ _____. I know You understand because You know I'm human, and not seeing where we're going, I feel _____

_____. But I know You love me and Your plans for me are for good, not for evil, so as I ride with You, Jesus, I'll give my best to _____

_____

_____, and I'm leaning on You, holding on to Your character and love, and asking You to _____

_____

_____. When I start to lean, slip, get tired or want to quit and go home, please

_____

_____. Thank You that You "know my frame" and You love me even in my weakness, as well as in my strength. I need Your renewing strength to _____

_____

_____. Thank You that You won't quit on me! In Jesus's name, amen! Holy Spirit, I'm listening.

_____

Cotton Candy Daddy

My big brother and I walked with Dad in the deepening twilight. I was four, Dave was eleven, and Dad had taken us to the small carnival in our little town for some fun after dinner. Tongue out, I happily lapped in the pink strands of cotton candy from the paper cone in my right hand, my eyes more on the sticky confection than on where I was walking. Suddenly Dad stopped, and I ran—*smack*—pink sugar and all, into his gray wool dress pants. With horror, I saw the wet wad of candy sticking to Dad's trousers and felt instant pangs of accountability—yes, even four-year-olds can feel responsible for their actions.

Dad turned as tears sprang into my eyes, but the only words from his gentle heart were, "Uh-oh! We'll have to clean that when we get home. It's okay, Rosie." My giant of a hero was heroically there for me again. I have absolutely no memory of any ridiculing, blaming, or invalidating words ever coming from my father (or my mother, for that matter). Dad never bubbled over with affection—he was a quiet man by nature—but he was always quietly, warmly present, accepting, forgiving, encouraging, and welcoming.

I don't remember if I ran into Dad and Mom's bedroom in the mornings or in the evenings, but I do remember climbing up on their bed when I was five with the jolly request, "Make a hill, Daddy!" He'd bend his knees in bed and obligingly let me slide down his legs. I wish in later years I'd asked him what he thought of this silly game; his answer might have surprised me with what it meant to him. And I wish I'd had the insight to tell him how much he influenced my understanding and perception of God as Father.

Rarely have I thought of God as a mean, hard master just waiting for this child to mess up so He could denigrate me and put me in my place. Frankly, only the insults and blame from a person whose opinion I valued more than any other have pushed me into shame and cries to God for His mercy. Did God tell me, "You're just not doing it for me?" No, but a man with a huge father wound did, and in recent years, I've seen what damage the father wound does in young hearts, spirits, and even literally in developing young brains.

Gordon Dalbey of the Abba Father Men's Ministry writes:

> No pain strikes more deeply into a man's heart than being abandoned emotionally and/or physically by Dad. No pain, therefore, more directly beckons the saving power of Father God. [11]

> See, I will send you the prophet Elijah before that great and dreadful day of the LORD comes. He will turn the hearts of the fathers to their children, and the hearts of the children to their fathers; or else I will come and strike the land with a curse.
>
> Malachi 4:5-6

Because the father wound is so destructive, Satan, the enemy of our soul—our mind, will, and emotions—and the father of lies, is "hell-bent" to hide the truth of this destructive wound and twist, pervert, deny the fatherhood of God and leave a man, as Dalbey states, "divorced from his destiny."

> You belong to your father, the devil, and you want to carry out your father's desires. He was a murderer from the beginning, not holding to the truth, for there is no truth in him. When he lies, he speaks his native language, for he is a liar and the father of lies.
>
> John 8:44

Crushing criticism kills; dismissing identity and value kills; abandonment kills. The father wound impacts daughters as well as sons, depriving girls of their inherent dignity, beauty, and value, boys of their integrity, courage, strength, and answer to Father God's call to servant-hearted brave leadership in their lives.

Because I knew my father admired me and loved me, in my teen years, no way would I allow a boy to take advantage of me. Years later, in response to a man who asked why I didn't immediately hold his hand and give him a kiss on our first date, I replied that holding a man's hand, and even more so, giving a kiss, meant something to me, and I didn't give either expression of affection and trust casually or without sincerity. A man had to show me his character to receive my proffered hand. My lips were—and are—sacred ground.

Fathers play a vital role in their children's ability to connect with God, their heavenly Father, as well as with other people. I loved a man with a huge, unrecognized, and denied father wound in his life. Neglect and callous comments from his father short-circuited the emotional wiring in his developing brain and sent signals of insecurity and invalidation that set up static in his spirit that impacted his ability to feel attachment with God. The empty heart he held up in his hands to his earthly father left him mistrusting his heavenly Father's intentions toward him as well. No amount of my affirming that God did love him and value him, that he was a creative and capable person I admired and God cherished, could make up for the hurt in his heart and spirit. The wound from his emotionally absent father put a distorted filter over the eyes of his understanding, and he began to view God as a big disappointment.

I'm certain that my intimate relationship with my earthly father helped me see God's hand evident in my life nearly every day. God wasn't in the trees, but trees bore God's fingerprints, trees were of God, just as the dollhouse my father made for me was of my earthly father's love, and the train layout he made for my brother was of his love. How many hours did my dad put into carving "bricks" in the block of wood that became a "fireplace," wiring my dollhouse, so the lights truly worked, cutting real shingles into tiny squares to roof my dollhouse? How many hours did he spend laying track and making plaster mountains and tunnels for my brother's train?

You may not have experienced such love and relationship with your own father. Even if your earthly father was cold, distant, or not even in the picture in your family, you do have an eternal Father who loves you and wants to be intimately connected and active in your life. How many hours did God, Your Father and Abba, too, spend creating you in your mother's womb? How gentle has He been when we "run into His pants" with our sticky messes, simply inviting us into a relationship while He cleans up the messes we make or helps us as we gather up the courage to admit our wrongs and mistakes to the people we've wounded and ask for their forgiveness?

The most profound memory I have of my father, even beyond all the wonderful times I spent with him in childhood, was one Sunday evening when I was thirty. Dad came out of the sanctuary after watching the Focus on the Family film series that I, as family ministries coordinator, had set up at our church and quietly, simply, broadly smiling, said, "Rosie, I love you."

Perhaps you know someone with a deep father wound. Perhaps you carry a deep father wound that you've never been able to honestly admit before. Perhaps you're a man and realize now that you unknowingly, out of your own wounding, created father wounds in your children and don't know how to clean up that mess. Perhaps you view Father God through a distorted lens of that disappointment, mistrust, and deep longing for unconditional love. The wonderful thing about our Father God is that when we lift our sticky hands and messes to Him, He turns and bends down to embrace us with His smiling, approving, limitless, healing, joyful love.

> For this reason I kneel before the Father, from whom every family in heaven and on earth derives its name. I pray that out of his glorious riches he may strengthen you with power through his Spirit in your inner being, so that Christ may dwell in your hearts through faith. And I pray that you, being rooted and established in love, may have power, together with all the Lord's holy people, to grasp how wide and long and high and deep is the love of Christ, and to know this love that surpasses knowledge—that you may be filled to the measure of all the fullness of God.

Ephesians 3:14-19

See what great love the Father has lavished on us, that we should be called children of God! And that is what we are! The reason the world does not know us is that it did not know him. Dear friends, now we are children of God, and what we will be has not yet been made known. But we know that when Christ appears, we shall be like him, for we shall see him as he is. All who have this hope in him purify themselves, just as he is pure [...] This is how we know that we live in him and he in us: He has given us of his Spirit. And we have seen and testify that the Father has sent his Son to be the Savior of the world. If anyone acknowledges that Jesus is the Son of God, God lives in them and they in God. And so we know and rely on the love God has for us. God is love. Whoever lives in love lives in God, and God in them.

1 John 3:1-3, 4:13-16

A "but" to pray: Father God, may I call You Daddy? I know sometimes I've pushed You off and held You at arm's length because I thought You were/would _____

_____ if I did what I wanted to do and ran into Your arms. If your father wasn't compassionate, be honest here: God, my own father _____ _____ out of his own humanity and wounds. _Or_ if you had a compassionate father, thank You that my own earthly father _____

_____

_ out of his human love. Abba, yes, I've made mistakes, and I "ran into Your pants" when I _____ _____. Thank You that You walk me home to simply clean up the mess. I made an even bigger mess when I _____

_____,

and I confess that I thought that would end Your acceptance and love for me. I was wrong! You can't deny Your nature, and Your nature and character are love, so Father, Daddy, Abba, I run to you today and say _____

_____

_____. You call me Your beloved child, period! Help me walk in the security of Your love as I _____ _____. In the name of Your beloved Son, my Savior, the lover of my soul, Jesus, who made me clean to be Your very own cherished child, amen! Holy Spirit, I'm listening.

_____

DAY 34

Strike the Rock

Perseverance. No visible results. Twenty-five years.
How long could you endure? When would frustration
overtake your faith? And was this a word God intended
for me?

Recently I visited the area headquarters for a missions organization sending humanitarian workers
to indigenous people in Mexico. Paper banners hung
along the walls of a large multi-purpose room. One col-
or indicated New Testament translations completed,
one color indicated translations underway, and just a
few of a third color targeted languages remaining to
have Bible translation underway. Those weren't just
banners; those were life stories, joys, tears, sacrifice, ill-
nesses overcome, dangers faced, loneliness for families
far away, children growing up isolated from their home
culture and friends and extended families, miracles,
healings, minds given the gift of literacy, the good news
of Jesus planted in hearts and lives, a chronicle of lives
invested over decades to bring hope, vision, humani-

tarian aid, and God's Word in their own heart language to how many hundreds of thousands of people.

If we were there, doing their work, pushing through, going without, threatened by local shamans and witch doctors, how long would we persevere before we saw "results"? One man asked that after twenty-five years of his and his wife's befriending, helping, giving into lives in the village, learning the language, and writing book after book of the Bible to give the villagers the hope of Jesus. Though they'd made friends in the village and the people truly appreciated all they had sacrificed and given, twenty-five years passed, and not a single person accepted Jesus as Lord. The local witch doctor had over the years threatened the villagers that if anyone embraced Jesus, he would put a spell of death upon them.

Had all their work been for nothing? I know I'd be asking that question, ready to pack up my family and belongings and head home deep in doubt that God had actually called me to that work. Deep in confusion and nearing despair, one day, the man experienced a vivid dream. He was standing in front of a large boulder, and a hammer lay on the ground. An angel walked up to the man and told him, "God wants you to strike the rock." Obediently the man began hammering away at the hard rock. He hammered, and hammered, and hammered, and hammered. Not a single chip flaked off the rock, not a single crack appeared in the hard, resistant surface. Tired and confused, the man put the hammer down.

Up walked the angel again, this time with a question, "What are you doing?"

The man poured out his exhausted frustration, saying, "The rock won't break!"

Then the angel kindly asked him a pointed question: "What did God tell you to do?"

"Strike the rock," the man replied.

"God didn't tell you to break the rock," the angel explained simply. "He just asked you to strike it."

Revelation and validation flashed into the weary man's mind and spirit. He and his wife had done exactly what they were sent to do, regardless of the results they did or didn't see!

They moved on to a neighboring village, and almost immediately, people began accepting Jesus as their Lord. What in the world was the difference, the couple wondered. Villagers explained matter-of-factly, "We aren't under the power of their witch doctor. He can't put a curse on us!" So many came to Christ that a church was planted in the second village. Not long after, the witch doctor in the neighboring village died, and Christians from the second village came to the ones of the first and led them to faith in Jesus, planting a church there as well. What truly did all their years of love and labor invested in that first village? Make the rock ready to crumble at just the right time!

How many of my prayers seem to have gone unheard and unanswered? Is it possible that God has asked me simply to "strike the rock"? Are my fervent prayers truly more effective than I know, than I see now?

> Then Jesus told his disciples a parable to show them that they should always pray and not give up. He said: "In a certain town there was a judge who neither feared God nor cared what people thought. And there was a widow in that town who kept coming to him with the plea, 'Grant me justice against my adversary.' "For some time he refused. But finally he said to himself, 'Even though I don't fear God or care what people think, yet because this widow keeps bothering me, I will see that she gets justice, so that she won't eventually come and attack me!'"
> And the Lord said, "Listen to what the unjust judge says. And will not God bring about justice for his chosen ones, who cry out to him day and night? Will he keep putting them off? I tell you, he will see that they get justice, and quickly. However, when the Son of Man comes, will he find faith on the earth?"
>
> Luke 18:1-8

Make sure that nobody pays back wrong for wrong, but always strive to do what is good for each other and for everyone else [...] always, pray continually, give thanks in all circumstances; for this is God's will for you in Christ Jesus.

1 Thessalonians 5:15-18

"Let us not become weary in doing good, for at the proper time we will reap a harvest if we do not give up" (Galatians 6:9).

I've thrown my "hammer" of prayer and hope down in exhaustion and frustration more than once, and I know I've lost some blessings out of sheer sorrow in not seeing immediate results. What blessing did I miss? What did I give up? How about you? What good are you weary of doing? Um, okay...has anyone seen my hammer? Let's persevere together!

A "but" to pray: God, I've prayed and prayed repeatedly for _____ , and it looks like nothing at all has happened, no answer is coming. Show me if I need to simply persevere in "striking the rock" or if it is time to move on, trusting that You will _____ when I keep on doing good in _____ _____. Give me the grace and strength to persevere in _____

___ or the grace to let go of _____. I will let You be God and Lord of the results! In Jesus's name, amen. Holy Spirit, I'm listening.

The Bug Blessed Me

Feeling my way from chair to chair in the darkness, I sat down next to someone in church on Wednesday night, perplexed by a cryptic voice message on my phone from the bargain travel site I'd booked my mission trip to Thailand through: "Go online immediately to view your reservation." I was set to fly to Thailand the next Tuesday with a suitcase stuffed with donated card-making supplies to take to a missionary conference. I'd done the same thing two years earlier, intending to give a "girls' night out" to women from all over the globe, but the response from men, women, and children who'd flooded the dining room and cut, glued, and stamped with delight had absolutely stunned me. I was fueled and fired to take the blessing back again.

Set and eager to start praising and packing that night, I suddenly sensed my body's churning "voice message," alerting me that lunch wasn't the only thing in my stomach; an unwelcome "bug" was growing. Oh, no! Not the flu a week before my flight! Nausea growing, I finally left the service and called my boss on my way home, "Dean, I won't be in first thing in the morning. I hope it's a twenty-four-hour bug, and I can come in late." Once home, I quickly brought up the email and, to my confusion, read two conflicting flight times into Seoul: one arriving forty-five minutes before my connecting flight, but another arriving just fifteen minutes before the flight to Bangkok.

Maybe, I thought, *My head and intestines will be calmer by morning,* so I curled up with a hot water bottle, a cup of ginger tea and prayed for healing.

I felt worse in the morning, but I called the travel site. What I heard filled me with panic. "The airline changed flight times, so we've canceled your itinerary."

"No!" I blurted over waves of nausea. "I made the reservation months ago, and I have to be in Bangkok for a conference."

Oblivious to my alarm, the agent said I could rebook my flight for only $3,000 more. "That won't work," I replied in a calm I didn't feel. "Can you please call the airline?" That began a four-hour fencing match, the agent thrusting they were only a broker, me parrying with, "Please call the airline." She did, and I prayed ferociously between holds and offers, declaring every scripture I knew about God being my shield and sword of victory.

Could I leave next month? Could I leave in two weeks? Could I go to another destination? No, no, no!

During the hold times, I lay on the floor and prayed, decreed, over myself:

"It may be that the LORD will look upon my misery and restore to me his covenant blessing instead of his curse today" (2 Samuel 16:12).

"All this is for your benefit, so that the grace that is reaching more and more people may cause thanksgiving to overflow to the glory of God" (2 Corinthians 4:15).

The agent's insensitivity churned frustration in my stomach on top of the bilious "bug," and her tide of consternation rose higher with my relentless requests to try again. Desperate, I finally pleaded, "Let me call the airline then; just *don't cancel my reservation!*"

> "No weapon formed against you shall prosper, And every tongue which rises against you in judgment You shall condemn. This is the heritage of the servants of the LORD, And their righteousness is from Me," Says the LORD.
>
> Isaiah 54:17 (NKJV)

The agent, glad to get rid of me, gave me a phone number, which turned out to be the airline's air cargo line. They transferred me to an agent, and twenty minutes later, God airdropped a miracle into my lap: the airline took responsibility for the schedule change and offered that if I could leave on Monday night and stay one extra day, they'd put me up for the day in a hotel in Seoul, so I could make my connecting flight to Bangkok!

"And we know that in all things God works for the good of those who love him, who have been called according to his purpose" (Romans 8:28).

Hooray for God and an upset stomach! I needed those four morning hours to battle bureaucracy and for God to bless me via the most unusual means He's ever used in my life. The "mess" made a miracle that blessed me with time in Seoul to walk, shower, eat lunch, and nap before my flight, a day to get over jetlag, and a day at the end of the conference to stay with friends in Chiang Mai whom I hadn't seen in over ten years!

In one more miracle, the "someone" I sat beside in church when the battle began was my friend Judy, who asked if the missionary ladies would like bracelets. "I couldn't help you the last time you went, so I'd like to help you now," she sweetly offered. Two days later, I discovered a box at my doorstep containing fifty lovely costume jewelry bracelets for the missionary women and girls and $500 to help pay for my flight!

"Oh, God," I gratefully cried on the other side of the world as one more time women and girls (with beautiful bracelets adorning their arms), and men and boys stamped, glued, cut, and created wonderful cards and bookmarks, "You did so much more than I could have ever dreamed, planned, done, or imagined!"

Thank You, God, for the bug in my belly that brought blessing beyond belief! Thank You that You reign as God, King, Provider, Healer, Lover, and Lord over my life despite my circumstances!

A "but" to pray: Most Merciful God! How many times, I wonder, have You diverted a scheme of Satan in my life, and I never even recognized Your hand was in the blessing, even in what looked like a calamity? Remind me now of a time when things looked black, *but You*, my God, came through for me and made a wonderful way for me to prosper _____

_____

_____. What circumstance right now do You want me to offer up to You to transform into a blessing or to see in the light of Your grace and possibilities? _____

_____

___. Thank You, thank You, Loving God, and help me trust You in days ahead that You *can* cause all things to work together for my good. In Jesus's name, amen. Holy Spirit, I'm listening.

_____

Ask Only If You Mean It

Only if you want to stretch your heart and carry the love...

Only if you're willing to sit beside Jesus, feel His anguish, fill in the names of those you love, and cry out with Him as He says, "Jerusalem, Jerusalem, [_____ _____] you who kill the prophets and stone those sent to you, how often I have longed to gather your children together, as a hen gathers her chicks under her wings, and you were not willing" (Matthew 23:37).

Oh, the relentless heart of God! Seven years ago, I asked Jesus to give me His heart for my beloved when I felt my feelings for him slipping. I knew it was wrong to let my heart's flame burn low, and I knew it was my responsibility to "guard your heart, for it is the well-spring of life" (Proverbs 4:23). It was my mission, my charge, my responsibility alone to guard my heart and thoughts. Ironically, that process began in me before the deepest betrayal of my life, and I'm grateful it did. I learned two important truths: (1) no one else can kill your heart, but you can and do when you poison it with resentment, unforgiveness, selfishness, believing your own misperceptions, focusing on bitterness, and contempt, and (2) don't ask Jesus for His heart for someone unless you want a relentless, *regardless* love implanted in you that lays down your own wounds to look deeply into the inmost heart of the life of another and value that person with love and forgiveness that *will not* be quenched, period.

I looked up Matthew Henry's commentary on Matthew 23:34-39 online at christianity.com and found this sadly still all too true analysis:

> Our Lord declares the miseries the inhabitants of Jerusalem were about to bring upon themselves, but he does not notice the sufferings he was to undergo. A hen gathering her chickens under her wings is an apt emblem of the Savior's tender love to those who trust in him, and his faithful care of them. He calls sinners to take refuge under his tender protection, keeps them safe, and nourishes them to eternal life. The present dispersion and unbelief of the Jews, and their future conversion

to Christ, were here foretold. Jerusalem and her children had a large share of guilt, and their punishment has been signal. But ere long, deserved vengeance will fall on every church that is Christian in name only. In the mean time [sic] the Saviour stands ready to receive all who come to him. There is nothing between sinners and eternal happiness, but their proud and unbelieving unwillingness.[12]

Jesus's disregard for His own coming agony comes from, and reveals, *that blazing passion for us* that bared Jesus's back and stretched out His hands to take the insults, taunts, scourge, and the nails and say, "Father, forgive them, for they don't know what they are doing." Love like that, in those circumstances, at the hands of betrayers and despisers? "You have to be kidding me" is what "rational" people who look out for themselves say. Look out for yourself, do what feels good, and move on and cut your losses when it doesn't. That's what most rational people claim and advise to be in mental and emotional health. But a note to us in the self-preserving, "self-actualizing," self-focused, personally validating narcissistic culture that is rapidly consuming our country and the world: some choices are not good, period.

Look out for yourself? That's not what I hear Jesus say, and this is where it gets hard and in your paradigm:

> You have heard that it was said, "Love your neighbor and hate your enemy." *But* I tell you: Love your enemies and pray for those who persecute you, that you may be sons [and daughters] or your Father in heaven.
>
> Matthew 5:43-45, emphasis mine

Do what feels good for *you*. I recall two neighbor boys taunting me in what I thought was a congenial game of "keep away," throwing the ball in high arcs far above my head as I tried pointlessly to catch the ball while one said, "She can't catch it! She's just a girl!" I remember the two older boys who held me under in the deep end of the community pool when I was nine years old. I'm guessing it felt good to them to exercise their power and watch me flail. I frankly thought I was going to die.

That's what we do to each other, sometimes on purpose, more often unintentionally (that would be me in some dumb mistakes): we step on others to lift our fragile egos higher. We taunt, we withhold, we use, we hold onto hurts and lash out and lacerate others, we exercise our rights and power, want our way and our ends by any means necessary to preserve what we think feels good for us. We see the leak in the boat and decide to take the one life vest and slide overboard instead of helping plug the hole; we look at the one—okay, even two—engine(s) out in a four-engine plane, put on a parachute, and bail out, rather than putting our body weight to the rudder alongside the pilot to land the plane safely and make the needed repairs.

But the heart of Jesus is relentless, and He comes up loving even after being held under by our "I'm perfectly capable of and justified in, and frankly enjoy, doing life *my* way, thank you very much." He was betrayed and despised then, and we still do it to Him now, *but He did what was faithfully loving anyway* and came up gloriously victorious, forgiving and giving and breaking down the walls that kept us from the longing to receive arms of God. Love doesn't always feel good. *How totally irrational!*

Yes, God's love *is irrational*—why on earth would *He* give Himself for the messes that are us—which makes up a huge chunk of what makes God holy, and wholly righteous and good and pure, wholly matchless, wholly unfathomable, and wholly breathtaking.

"But God demonstrates his own love for us in this: While we were still sinners, Christ died for us" (Romans 5:8).

Irrational? Absolutely! He plugged the hole in the boat; *He* put His weight to the rudder of the plane, all for an unbroken, eternal, joyous relationship with us.

Oh, yes, I'm codependent: dependent on Jesus, this Love Incarnate, for my next heartbeat and breath, holding His hand for dear life as I go into the future single, with no hope of ever being able to earn enough to support myself, and glad to wrap the tassels of my prayer shawl, His "wings," His promises, around my hands clasped by His as the hands of bride and bridegroom are bound together in the wedding ceremony. God binds Himself to you; is that a thought to set your head and heart and rationality reeling? The Creator who spoke infernos of stars and dark matter and gravity and neutrinos and optic nerves and DNA and embryos into existence binds Himself to you when you come to Him through Jesus. God binds Himself to you! Then He has the audacity to call you *Hephzibah* (delighted in) and Beulah (chosen) and rejoices over you! (See Isaiah 62: 3-5.)

So go ahead and ask for that heart but be prepared to receive a passionate, unquenchable love for those who've done you wrong and for the lost and broken. It will hurt. Don't you think Jesus's heart is capable of sorrow? If that prospect offends you, don't even ask Jesus for His heart for another person! But if you dare to, what He gives you in return is a heart free from bitterness, contempt, pride, anger, unforgiveness, and all the wounds that chained you to the pain of offenses.

Did it get me my husband back? No, but if Jesus had asked me to be Hosea, I would have been and would have rejoiced. Jesus had another way for me, so I do choose to rejoice. Go figure when you dare to ask Jesus for His heart. It may be out of love that He sometimes won't give us what we want, so He can give us what's best. I rejoice that my heart is bound by and to the promise of my kinsman redeemer Boaz, Jesus Himself, and His gift to me of a piece of His precious, a word far too small for his indescribable, fiery love.

> Dear friends, let us love one another, for love comes from God. Everyone who loves has been born of God and knows God. Whoever does not love does not know God, because God is love [...] This is love: not that we loved God but that he loved us and sent his Son as an atoning sacrifice for our sins. Dear friends, since God so loved us, we also ought to love one another. No one has ever seen God, *but* if we love one another, God lives in us and his love is made complete in us.
>
> 1 John 4:7-8, 10-12, emphasis mine

Beloved, as John the Beloved would say, that's a risk worth taking and a love worth bearing.

A "but" to pray: Father God, Your Word says that if I delight myself in You, You will give me the desires of my heart. Does that always mean I get what I want, or does it sometimes mean You will put new desires, Your desires, for me into my heart? I'm asking about that because in my heart, _____

_____

_____, but I also want what You want for me. You know how hard it is for me to fell or act lovingly toward

_____

_____, *but* I want to have Your heart for _____ _____. If You give me Your heart for that person, I need Your help beside me and inside me to know how to truly love in the way that's best for them and in the ways that are best for me, also. Teach me how to love as You love, Jesus. Gosh, did I just ask that? I know You do want me to have Your heart for others and to see them through Your eyes, so I'm asking today for Your help to _____

_____.

Thank You, Father God, for conforming me to be more like Jesus because You *love* me! Hang in there with me! In Jesus's name, amen! Holy Spirit, I'm listening.

_____

I Think, Therefore...I Dance!

God heard my heart cry and answered with His blessing powerfully and surprisingly!

I picked myself up off the floor after yet another sudden tragedy in my life. How much more could I take? After a tragic divorce, now I faced this tragic death? I knew the enemy of my soul wanted to take me out, end my life, end my trust and faith in God, but somehow I found the strength to rise up and say out loud, "God, I'm going to believe *You still love me, You still have good ahead for me, and this is not for my destruction!*" I walked over to the computer, went to my email, and to my astonishment, I saw a message from the Christian dating site I'd been on for years. I'd let my subscription expire when I met "Ken18" months earlier. We were married just eight months when the second tragedy, a DUI driver plowing into him on his bicycle along with a group of ten cyclists, stopped in the bike lane at a red light, took Ken's life and the life of another cyclist. Now, six weeks later, I gathered my strength to believe God still cared about me.

I clicked on the email, went to the dating site, and to my amazement, there was my profile, still up! And I had a message from a man named Daniel, who wrote, "I like what you say about the Bible's book of Ruth in your profile. I'd like to meet you for lunch sometime." I was first amazed that my profile was still active on the site and even more amazed to read Daniel's message and his profile. I'm the mom of a missionary, and Daniel's profile said he was on the missions board of Green Valley Presbyterian Church! I went to the church website just to check this out, and sure enough, there was Daniel's name on the missions board.

"God, is this You?" I asked. I gathered my quivering faith and courage and responded to Daniel's message to me, giving him my phone number.

A few days later, we met at a nice local restaurant for lunch. My first thought was, *What a tall man! And what a warm smile he has!* Over lunch, we discovered that we had many things in common in our lives. We were both born in Indiana, about a hundred miles apart, a year apart, into families with solid Christian parents and grandparents. At age four, each of us saw the paper fan from a funeral home in the back of the church pew in front of us with a picture of Jesus holding a lamb, and we each knew Jesus was telling us He loved us! My father built an apartment on the back of our house for his widowed mother to live in. Seven years before we met, Daniel left a lucrative job as a vice president of a mortgage company to come out to Green Valley to take care of his widowed mother. My parents were caring, giving Christians. Daniel's grandmother bought food and took it to the Native Americans on a reservation near Tucson. His father, who owned some grocery stores, bought food from his own stores to give to hungry people in his town. Several times I'd bought chicken and other food for my neighbor's family since they only had money to buy rice and beans. Daniel himself volunteered at a food bank and drove to local farms to buy and pick up excess produce from local farmers to give to the food bank. Daniel lost his only sister to cancer the year before we met and lost his beloved mother just weeks before our first lunch date.

We'd both just about given up on ever finding a true Christian to spend our lives with. In fact, Daniel had nearly decided to resign himself to being alone forever and moving back to Indiana when he saw my profile on the dating site. *Holey socks!* I thought and asked, "Did we come from the same family?" Daniel smiled, answered yes, and pointed his finger straight up toward heaven.

Long story short, we went to church together and had lunch and chatted for about five weeks, when Daniel said to me one day, "I don't want to date you anymore... I want to marry you!"

Startled, I didn't answer immediately but told him I'd pray about it. Shortly after this, Daniel drove back to

Indianapolis to photograph a wedding and asked me if I'd fly back and meet him there. I prayed, and early the next morning, God literally rolled me out of bed with the words "Pay attention to this!" ringing in my spirit. I booked a flight, called Daniel, gave him the details, and the next day flew to meet him. I enjoyed meeting his friends and hearing their appreciation for Daniel's integrity and kindness. We drove back to Arizona together, chastely staying in separate motel rooms when we stopped overnight.

Short story short, the pastor of the Green Valley Presbyterian Church, which Daniel's grandparents helped find, married us not long afterward. Whirlwind courtship? Yes. God's hand guiding us both, assuring us this was God's will and plan? Yes! Now, five years later, we've discovered even more things in common. Daniel's maternal grandfather, a professional oil painter, painted a picture of the old mission church at Tumacácori. My paternal grandmother, who painted for a hobby, painted a watercolor painting of the same perspective of the same mission church! For our first Christmas, I found a set of old paper fans on a website, bought them, and gave them to Daniel, and yes, one was the fan with the painting of Jesus holding a lamb, the same picture we'd both seen when we were four!

I still sometimes ask God why the roads that led Daniel and me together went through valleys of grief and pain, but we both are sure that God's great mercy, love, grace, goodness, and faithfulness brought us together.

"Even though I walk through the valley of the shadow of death, I will fear no evil, for You are with me; Your rod and your staff, they comfort me" (Psalm 23:4, NASB).

There in the basket in the kitchen stands the fan with Jesus, our Good Shepherd and your Good Shepherd, who saw these two lonely, sad "lambs" and brought us together in His green, blessing-filled pasture! Yes, God loves you! Trust His love!

A "but" to pray: Lord, beautiful Savior, my loving Father God, help me hope and trust and believe in Your love, Your ability and willingness to hear my heart cries and answer them in Your time out of Your great love and grace, with blessings and goodness for me. You've heard me cry out _____

_____

_____, and You know I've nearly lost hope, *but* help me trust You *will answer me* out of Your goodness, in Your time, Your will and way, and help me hang onto *You*, so I can _____

_____.

I want to know You fully. I sometimes have trouble with _____ in my relationship with You. I can get too caught up in _____. Help me, Loving God, to both know You and experience You. Holy Spirit, come into my life and do what I can't do for myself. If I could ask You for one thing in my relationship with You if You were sitting right here beside me, I'd ask You to give me more _____

_____. Thank You that You *want* me to know and to experience more of You and Your love and care and power every day! Right now, in the privacy of my own space, I'm choosing to let myself _____

_____ out of pure delight in You, even if in this moment, it feels more like sacrifice than privilege. Abba God, thanks for Your goodness coming into my life. In Jesus's name, amen! Holy Spirit, I'm listening.

_____

_____ Lead me in this adventure of my life, calm the stormy seas, or enable me to walk with You upon them. Let me bear the image of Jesus in all I think, do, and say. Father God, lead me on, my Lord, my God, my Savior, my Healer, my Counselor, my Guide, my Enabler, my Redeemer, my Father! In Jesus's name, amen!

Know Your Real Enemy, Seize Your Real Victory

An eating machine: emotionless, calculating, seeking to fill its own desires and satisfy its hunger. Simple. Prey is prey, no personal agenda other than a full stomach. Horrifying truth if you're a gazelle: it's not about you; it's about the lion's hunger.

I came face-to-face with a horrifying corollary revelation as I awakened from a dream at five o'clock one morning. In my dream, someone I loved and trusted was dispassionately humiliating me. The conversation was about, of all things, a cell phone plan, but that was beside the point I suspect the Holy Spirit was trying to impress upon me. I woke with a feeling of stark horror, seeing an image of the person I knew calmly driving a knife into my chest while he spoke with cold, dispassionate, conscienceless, emotionless, heartless, impersonal, calculated deliberation about why he was doing it.

I have always hated violent, scary movies. I have a natural empathy for others, and I always identified with characters in movies, whether with their joy or their terror. I have to be careful about what I let into my overly compassionate brain! The most frightening movies and real-life stories involve killers—and in these days, terrorists—who take other lives in that impersonal, passionless, conscienceless, remorseless, deliberate, cold, and calculated way. They don't kill because they are angry with their victim; they kill to satisfy a hunger within themselves that is the embodiment of pure evil.

I immediately asked the Lord what in the world my dream was about, and suddenly I knew. Our enemy, the devil, doesn't care about and isn't the least bit interested in us as individuals; his only interest is in hurting God, depriving God of the objects of His love, the ones Jesus cherishes, the ones who return His love with gladness and praise and worship. Satan's hunger is to destroy God's creation, God's children, and God's purposes for their lives and relationship with Him.

"Be self-controlled and alert. Your enemy the devil prowls around like a roaring lion looking for someone to devour" (1 Peter 5:8).

Finally, be strong in the Lord and in his mighty power. Put on the full armor of God, so that you can take your stand against the devil's schemes. For our struggle is not against flesh and blood, but against the rulers, against the authorities, against the powers of this dark world and against the spiritual forces of evil in the heavenly realms. Therefore put on the full armor of God.

Ephesians 6:10-13

I remembered another odd incident when I was seventeen years old. One evening, I was taking a shower when suddenly, out of nowhere, the thought of a universe without God struck me. The empty horror of barren, pointless, cold, and empty existence sank me to my knees, shivering on the tile under the warm running water. I shook off the panic by reminding myself of the love I knew from Jesus, the certainty that He lived, He loved, and died and rose again for me and lives forever vibrantly and gloriously still with an undying love for me.

Oh, how that must "fry" the devil when we know with heart-level, gut-level certainty how much the Creator of the universe cherishes us! Lucifer was the chief cherub, the leader of worship in heaven when he let love for his own beauty pollute his heart and set him resolutely and viciously against God Almighty and God's creation, including all of humanity. He and the angels who joined him, a third of the host of heaven who rebelled against God, were defeated and cast down, his name changed to Satan, which means "destruction."

How his narcissistic anger must burn in knowing his defeat is certain because of the victory Jesus won in taking upon Himself all our sins and our punishment on the cross, forever canceling our guilty verdict and restoring us to freely forgiven fellowship with our Father!

Do you know how precious you are? Do you know you were born onto a cosmic battlefield? The most important part you play in the battle for yourself is coming to know and believe the love God has for you (1 John 4:16).

The next strategic understanding we must have is that we do have an enemy who wants nothing more than to convince us the first truth isn't true. His weapons of temptation, accusation, and deception are limited and totally useless against our sure knowledge of the price God paid for us to live in fellowship with Him and our firm resolve to live, out of that love we know God has for us, lives that reflect love, joy, peace, patience, kindness, goodness, faithfulness, gentleness, and self-control (Galatians 5:22) even in the face of a narcissistic, self-focused, personal satisfaction-driven world, even in the face of other people who've been fed the lies, distortions, accusations, temptations, and abuses the devil lays out as a snare to snag them, capture them, then devour all of God's plans and purposes for them, in them, and through them.

And the only reason he conducts this hideous, horrifyingly impersonal, calculated, cold, heartless, conscienceless, passionless, brutal warfare is to hurt our Father God. I, for one, will not give my enemy the satisfaction of his perverted hunger. I choose to believe, in spite of the reality of wounding, disrespect, and dismissal in my life by others who seem to have no empathy, that the greater reality is this:

> How great is the love the Father has lavished on us, that we should be called children of God! And that is what we are! [...] He who does what is sinful is of the devil, because the devil has been sinning from the beginning. The reason the Son of God appeared was to *destroy the devil's work.* [...] This is how we know what love is: Jesus Christ laid down his life for us. And we ought to lay down our lives for our brothers [...] Dear friends, do not believe every spirit, but test the spirits to see whether they are from God [...] You, dear children, are from God and have overcome them, because

the one who is in you [Jesus] is greater than the one who is in the world [...] Dear friends, let us love one another, for love comes from God [...] This is love, not that we loved God, but that he loved us and sent his Son as an atoning sacrifice for our sins. Dear friends, since God so loved us, we also ought to love one another.

1 John 3:1, 8, 16; 4:4, 7-8, 10-11; emphasis mine

And so I choose to love everyone I can, in every way I can, at every time I can because I *am* part of the victory of Jesus, and I have a job to do in making His love real to others. I will not cave to bitterness, addictions, offenses, my own insecurity that might lead me to demand control, things my way, "worship" from others; I will not let the devourer use me to hurt my beloved, loving Father God! Once again, I come face-to-face with Jesus's words:

You have heard that it was said, "Love your neighbor and hate your enemy." But I tell you, love your enemies and pray for those who persecute you, that you may be children of your Father in heaven. He causes his sun to rise on the evil and the good, and sends rain on the righteous and the unrighteous. If you love those who love you, what reward will you get? Are not even the tax collectors doing that? And if you greet only your own people, what are you doing more than others? Do not even pagans do that? Be perfect, therefore, as your heavenly Father is perfect.

Matthew 5:43-48

You were *not* created to be the prey of a hungry, bitter, arrogant, and calculating enemy either; you were created to be loved by the Author of Life and the Lover of your soul and to live and love out of that love as deeply as you can, every day, trusting that your Father in heaven beams on you as you ask Him for the grace, insight, forgiveness, and strength to love as God loves! Rise up and claim that love for yourself, to wrap yourself in a fiery passion for you forever!

Know your enemy, seize your victory!

A "but" to pray: The world likes to pretend Satan is just a comic book character, and maybe I've fallen into that category, too, God. But here I am, face-to-face with the truth from the Bible, your Word, that I do have an enemy of my soul. *But* Jesus, *You* are the *Lover of my soul.* Because You are, and because You tell me, "You, _____, are of God, my child, and have overcome them because I who am in you am greater than he who is in the world," I choose to believe you. I thought _____ was my enemy, but I see behind _____ are lies and deceptions and wounding of the enemy in _____'s life, so I choose to pray for an end to the enemy's plans in _____, and I will choose to live and love out of the abundant, overflowing love You have for me, Abba God, Almighty! In Jesus's name, amen. Holy Spirit, I'm listening.

Spin Me Around the Stars

Crickets chirped in the warm summer night as I looked upward, expectantly waiting for my father to do what I'd longingly waited for. He lifted the long black tube of his hand-built telescope off its mount and set it delicately down in the soft grass. Darkness draped over us like a shawl, made lacy with the bright and faint punctuations of myriads of stars. Stars and planets were the awe of the evening, but my delight was in what sometimes happened next. My father swooped down, scooped me up, planted me gently on the flat mount atop his tripod, and spun me around. I looked up at the heavens in complete bliss as the stars whirled around me, covered with wonder and embraced in my father's love.

I don't think Dad ever knew how much what to him must have seemed just spontaneous silliness meant to me. He must have enjoyed it, though, because he did it many times. My father wasn't a man given to horseplay, merriment, or even much conversation. He surely must have said it while I was young, I think, but I don't remember hearing him say the words "I love you" until I was nearly thirty. I knew his love when I stood beside him at his bench in the garage as he helped me hammer nails into a board or click the Morse code key of his radio, or when I sat in his lap as he read the Sunday funnies to me. But I felt his love when he spun me around the stars.

Today, flat on my face on the floor, crying out to experience, to feel, the love of my heavenly Father, this whisper of a memory came to me. In the vastness of the throne room of heaven, surrounded by angelic hosts, bathed in the unapproachable light of the glory of God, knowing full well it's only because of Jesus, I have the audacity to ask God for what I'd love: for my Father to step down, scoop me up, plant me atop the mount of his hand-made "telescope," which is probably His very own hand, and spin me around the stars, covered with wonder and embraced in my Father's love.

I know, I know; we ought to have a holy reverential fear of God, and I do. But I have to wonder, does it delight God when His child longs for and has the faith to ask for a simple moment of a Father's "daddyness"? When His children delight in Him, in who He is, in His love? Delight pops up in many verses of scripture, so why do I feel guilty when I long to look for God's love to delight me? I know my earthly dad didn't take offense when I wanted to enjoy something special and Dad–daughter with him. Hmmm...Again I think on these wonderful living, resounding, still vibrant words of truth from God's own voice to men of centuries ago:

"The LORD delights in those who fear him, who put their hope in his unfailing love" (Psalm 147:11).

"The LORD your God is with you, he is mighty to save. He will take great delight in you, he will quiet

you with his love, he will rejoice over you with singing"
(Zephaniah 3:17).

"Delight yourself in the LORD, and he will give you
the desires of your heart" (Psalm 37:4, ESV).

Some people are privileged to know an outpouring
of fatherly love from their earthly fathers. Many more
don't. But I don't think we need to fear taking to our
heavenly Father that empty spot in our hearts that
needs the embrace of a daddy's spontaneous "silliness"/
joy. I understand that the writer of Hebrews was talking about our weakness and temptation when he wrote,
"Let us then approach the throne of grace with confidence, so that we may receive mercy and find grace to
help us in our time of need" (Hebrews 4:16), but I dare
to trust that we can approach the throne of grace with
confidence so that we can receive the lavish mercy of a
Father's delighted love.

"How great is the love the Father has lavished on us,
that we should be called children of God! And that is
what we are!" (1 John 3:1)

For now, it's a metaphor that brings me (and you
too, I pray) peace and encouragement to ask God for
experiences with Him that delight my soul, but I also
look forward expectantly to the day God, my Father, really does spin me around the stars!

A "but" to pray: Father God, I've been afraid sometimes to ask for an embrace from Your love. Sometimes
I've doubted You are willing to do that, but today I'm

going to trust that _____

_____. Sometimes I feel so far from Your love, and I think often it's my earthly perception of love based on my flawed experience, coupled with lingering "God of judgment" attitudes about You, that hold me back from truly knowing Your love. Where do those things inhibit my intimacy with You? _____

_____, *but* I dare to believe You meant it when You told the apostle Paul that nothing—not even my flawed attitudes—can separate me from the love of God that is in Christ Jesus, our Lord (Romans 8:38-39). So I have the faith-based audacity today to ask You to delight me with Your love, show me some spontaneous fatherly "silliness" that will mean the world to me, and help me delight, just purely delight, in You. How do you want to love me today? I expectantly wait. In Jesus's name, amen. Holy Spirit, I'm listening.

_____

Popsicles or Presence?

I'm amazed when I speak to a child or a child speaks to me, and I recognize a truth about God's character as our Father. I spent eighty minutes each week at the school where I worked tutoring Carl, whose native language wasn't English, in reading while his classmates had their Spanish lesson. The previous aide in his classroom advised me that the only way she'd been able to get Carl's cooperation in reading was to reward him with candy, so I continued her policy when I took over her position and "inherited" Carl and his reluctance to study.

As we walked down the hallway toward the school library for our last session of the semester, Carl began complaining that the students in Spanish class were having a party that day. "Why don't I get a treat? They're getting popsicles!" he demanded.

Using the "love and logic" approach to discipline, I returned a question. "Carl, do any of the other students in your class get candy for reading?"

"No."

"And what do you say when we go back to the classroom, and the other children ask why you got candy, and they didn't?"

Silence, a pout, and a glare from eyes hooded by his wrinkled brow.

Grudgingly Carl admitted they didn't get candy for reading, but he still was incensed at the "unfairness" of his situation. I could see words alone weren't going to open his eyes. Carl resentfully pulled out a chair at the library table and plopped down, his arms folded. I took out the log of our reading sessions and asked him, "Can you count by twos to help me count how many pieces of candy you've had since we started meeting together?"

"Two, four, six..." he counted as I kept turning pages in our log, "...eighty, eighty-two, eighty-four." In silence, I let that truth seep into his thinking before I asked, "How many treats do you think the other children are getting from the Spanish teacher? Eighty-four?"

"No," Carl admitted, and his uncrossed arms showed me he was beginning to get the message.

"Carl, you've had a party every day."

He sighed heavily. I understood his childish frustration that could only see how the other students were partying back in the classroom while I was asking him to read, something that felt like work to him.

"Carl, you can read any book you want to read today, even the easy Dr. Seuss books that you like so much."

I knew how he loved to read books with silly words and rhymes, and I saw the value in asking him to pick out rhyming words, including rhyming nonsense words, and make new rhymes with them. Even those books could be a challenge for his English fluency. Carl zoomed over to the shelf and brought back the easiest book he'd read this semester, no challenge to him now, but I knew he needed some joy and success on this day. He flew through the words. Then I offered what I knew would surprise him.

"Carl, why don't you choose a book you'd like me to read to you today?"

In disciplining with love and logic, you can't let only logic reign and omit the love. Carl chose a story we'd never read about a silly chicken in New York City, and I let the actor in me take the stage as I cackled the Yiddish text in a voice like a chicken.

But as I read, I was hearing a familiar voice in my heart reciting a story in the Bible I'd read many times about two brothers. The younger one took his inheritance early, left his work at his father's house, left home, and wasted his life and the money. The older brother wasn't at all happy when his brother returned, broken and truly sorry, and their father threw a lavish party.

> The older brother became angry and refused to go in [...] "But when this son of yours who has squandered your property with prostitutes comes home, you kill the fattened calf for him!" "My son," the father said, "you are always with me, and everything I have is yours."
>
> Luke 15:28, 30-31

How often I yell, "Unfair!" and feel I need a "treat" every time I see someone else blessed. Good grief, I already have the biggest, sweetest blessing: I get to live in my Father God's "house" every day, enjoying an intimate relationship with God's Holy Spirit and Jesus that is in itself a treat and treasure and party. Even when God's disciplining me, teaching me, and asking me to stretch and work, He showers me with unexpected provision, kind people in my life, and the rejoicing I feel when the love He promises me in the Bible takes root in my heart. Our Father is the party!

Why am I concerned about how other people who "do me dirty" seem to be enjoying today's "popsicle" when I've already inherited assuredly more than eighty-four blessings straight from my Father's love? How many times has God's spirit connected me wonderfully with someone who needed to hear of His love or with someone who had a word for me straight from God's heart to mine? Who's the one enjoying a party every day? Me!

"And I—in righteousness I will see your face; when I awake, I will be satisfied with seeing your likeness" (Psalm 17:15).

"You have made known to me the path of life; you will fill me with joy in your presence, with eternal pleasures at your right hand" (Psalm 16:11).

Right in the middle of a reading lesson, I reminded myself of verses in the most well-known and beloved psalm in the Bible:

> You prepare a table before me in the presence
> of my enemies; you anoint my head with oil;
> my cup overflows. Surely goodness and love
> will follow me all the days of my life, and I will
> dwell in the house of the LORD forever.
> Psalm 23:5-6

I gave Carl the rest of the bag of candy to take home. And guess what? The Spanish teacher gave him a popsicle, too.

The truth is none of the treats we gave could put a real hunger for learning into Carl or any of the students, nor did those things create a relationship with us as teachers, mentors, and friends. At some point, students need to come to the realization that learning—the transforming growth in them—*is the real reward* that comes out of time and relationship with the teacher.

That's easy to see when we look at children and the "reward everything with a carrot" mentality so prevalent in elementary education but are we, adults, so very different? We live in an "entitlement" culture, with happiness and success by the world's standards the primary reward for most of us if we truly examine our motives for work, spending, relationships, and even (if I dare to look deeply) our attitudes toward God, faith, and church. Did the writers of our Declaration of Independence intend the "pursuit of happiness" to be the goal and end game for the American people?

I'm not advocating poverty or unhappiness as virtues. But in the eternal scheme of things, could my bank account, anything under my roof, any vehicle, any place I vacation, any hobby or pursuit ever measure up to the abundant riches of knowing and dwelling in God's presence as His cherished child? Does anything I can buy come close to the security of His character as a mightily loving Father or take the place of His power to change me from who I am into who I can become, or replace the joy I can have when I let Him love me? Can anything displace or replace the real, lasting inner satisfaction and thrill I feel when I let Him love others through me in my day?

Yes, I know God is omnipresent, God is everywhere, but am I experiencing His present presence? How often do I really encounter God's presence? The times I have, I've been speechless. Can I honestly say I want His presence and His affirmation more than the "goodies" He, or the world, gives me?

> Draw near to God and He will draw near to you. Cleanse your hands, you sinners; and purify your hearts, you double-minded. Be miserable and mourn and weep; let your laughter be turned into mourning and your joy to gloom. Humble yourselves in the presence of the Lord, and He will exalt you.
>
> James 4:8-10 (NASB)

"Honor and majesty are [found] in His presence; strength and joy are [found] in His sanctuary" (1 Chronicles 16:27, AMPCE; brackets in the original).

"Satisfy us in the morning with your unfailing love, that we may sing for joy and be glad all our days" (Psalm 90:14).

I heard James MacDonald speak one evening at a large local church, and the point of his message riveted my attention on this one transcendent, transforming truth: what you and I and perhaps most of your loved ones, friends, and work associates never even realize they are missing is the manifest presence of God. We are so satiated with what we can grab and get for ourselves or what people and things can give to temporarily satisfy our longing for meaning and true identity that we've dulled our hunger for the true food we need: relationship with Almighty God.

In his book *Vertical Church: What Every Heart Longs For. What Every Church Can Be*, MacDonald writes:

> Most of the church landscape in my lifetime has been heavily invested in trying to do something for Jerry or Sherri or some other icon of unchurchness. The problem is that they have been only about themselves from the moment they could wail for their mothers, and the decision to give them at church what they can find in any self-help book appears now as a choice to abandon the One in whose honor the church gathers. What they need is to be set free from themselves with finality and to be lost in the awesome wonder of the manifest presence of God.[13]

Can I honestly cry out as David did with the same hunger, thirst, and longing for God Himself?

> You, God, are my God, earnestly I seek you; I
> thirst for you, my whole being longs for you,
> in a dry and parched land where there is no
> water. I have seen you in the sanctuary and
> beheld your power and your glory. Because
> your love is better than life, my lips will glo-
> rify you. I will praise you as long as I live, and
> in your name I will lift up my hands. I will
> be fully satisfied as with the richest of foods;
> with singing lips my mouth will praise you.
>
> Psalm 63:1-5

With an overflowing heart, I long to cry out to the
Father of love, "You are my celebration! Living in Your
love is my reward. Bring the lost ones home to know
You, too!" I am meant to encounter, know, and feast in
God's glory, transcendence, being, and passionate love.
How in the world can I earn, buy, accumulate around
me, or bask in the "glory" of anything that, in any way,
comes close to experiencing the living God?

A "but" to move: Father God, I confess I'm focused
on things more than I am on encountering and truly
knowing *You*. Help me truly know my deepest motives
and line up my desires with Your desires for me and
my relationship with You. Like a child, I get so angry
sometimes when people who don't honor You seem to
prosper or get victories and blessings that I don't, *but*

I'm reminding myself today if I draw near to You, You promise to come close to me. Really? *You are the party*, so I'll uncross my arms, lift up my eyes, and listen to You tell me, Your child that You want _____

_____. I want You in my life, truly, deeply, Father! Show me how and give me the hunger and thirst I need to truly want You. Make Your home in my heart and take me into the celebration of Your fatherly heart for me today! Holy Spirit, I'm listening, _____

_____

_____

_____, and thank You, Father God, for Your love through Jesus!

Blessings as you go on your own journey into God's heart,

Your fellow traveler,
Rose Hunter

Endnotes

1 Joyce Meyer, *Battlefield of the Mind* (FaithWords, 2017), 162.

2 Dallas Willard, *The Divine Conspiracy* (Harper Collins, 2009), 282–283.

3 John Barnett, vocalist, "Father of Lights," 2000, Doing the stuff, Mercy/Vineyard Publishing.

4 "The Minting Process Revealed," United States Mint, accessed May 12, 2021. http://sharedfiles.toolbox-forteachers.com/pbl/files/44ad5bb0-97aa-4bc7-bd5c-fbe222882806.pdf.

5 David Ruis, vocalist, "We Will Dance," 2003, track 13 on *This Is Love: 13 Powerful Worship Songs Celebrating the Cross*, Mercy/Vineyard Publishing (ASCAP).

6 "The Story of Sea Glass," American Craft Works, accessed May 12, 2021. http://www.americancraft-works.com/TheStoryofSeaglass.html.

7 Merriam-Webster, s.v. "Sacrament," accessed May 12, 2021. https://www.merriam-webster.com/dictionary/sacrament.

8 Stuart Townend, vocalist, "How Deep the Father's Love," 1990, track 9 on *Say The Word*, Thankyou Music (PRS).

9 Ibid.

10 Joseph Burgo, "What It's Really Like to Love a Narcissist," YourTango. Published August 3, 2020. https://www.yourtango.com/experts/joseph-burgo-phd/narcissist-love.

11 Gordon Dalbey, "Healing the Father-Wound: The Ultimate Men's Movement," AbbaFather, accessed June 2, 2021. https://www.abbafather.com/articles/article_hfw.pdf.

12 "Matthew Henry's Bible Commentary (concise)," Christianity.com, accessed May 12, 2021. https://www.christianity.com/bible/commentary.php?com=mhc&b=40&c=23.

13 James MacDonald, *Vertical Church: What Every Heart Longs for. What Every Church Can Be* (David C Cook, 2012), quoted in Goodreads, accessed June 9, 2021. https://www.goodreads.com/work/quotes/18391246-vertical-church-what-every-heart-longs-for-what-every-church-can-be.